TO THE TOP FROM NOWHERE

Sibusiso Vilane with Gail Jennings

Foreword by Sir Ranulph Fiennes

AARDVARK
PRESS

Aardvark Press Publishing (Pty) Ltd
PO Box 37571, Valyland 7978, Cape Town, South Africa

www.aardvarkpress.co.za

This book was printed in South Africa,
on paper that was produced from managed forests.

ISBN 978-0-9584907-8-8

Front cover images: Top panel, from top left, clockwise: Sibusiso in loinskins as a youth in Swaziland; at the base of Malolotja Falls in Swaziland; John Doble at Malolotja Falls; the Watt family, from left to right: Douglas, Kelly, Steven and Penny; John and Sibusiso in the Drakensberg, South Africa; Sibusiso on Ngwenya Mountain in Malolotja Nature Reserve; the queen of the Himalayas, Mount Everest; Sibusiso flanked by his benefactors, John Doble (left) and Everest south sponsor Adam Fleming (right); on top of the world, Sibusiso on Everest's summit with Robert Anderson (left) and David Hamilton (right).
Back cover images: From top left, clockwise: Sibusiso; Sibusiso with Base Camp north manager Gianni; Khumbu Icefall, Everest south (©Børge Ousland); Camp Two, Everest south (©Børge Ousland); above North Col (©Sibusiso Vilane).
Colour section: Individual photographers have been credited *in situ*.

Other photos ©Sibusiso Vilane.
If we have failed to credit any images appropriately we will be happy to make amends in the next printing.

www.sibusisovilane.com

Cover concept by Cornelle Ellis and
finishing by Damian Gibbs, Orchard Publishing (www.op.co.za).
Printed by Montage Print, cnr Glenluce and Glenavon Street, Glenesk, Johannesburg.

Dedication

This book is dedicated to my late mother.

Mum, you spent your lifetime striving so hard to take care of me and my late sister. You died very poor, a result of your dedication and commitment to raising us. You chose to have no food so that we could have an education, even though you had none. You always believed that one day I would be a good father and a man who was able to provide for my family. Thank you for being so positive. Because of you my eyes are open.

Contents

Foreword

I have enjoyed many travels in my life: from walking unaided across the Antarctic continent, to leading the first polar circumnavigation of the earth, to discovering a lost city in Oman ... but not until I met Sibusiso Vilane did I consider a high-altitude challenge such as Everest.

We first met in 2003 through our mutual friend, John Doble, and Sibu immediately impressed me with his optimism, enthusiasm and unfailing belief that failure should never be an option.

I was also greatly impressed by Sibu's determination to climb, to achieve, to explore, despite what anyone else might have to say about obstacles. He therefore didn't have to try too hard to persuade me to join him on his second Everest trip – to climb from the north side – in 2005.

As I write this foreword, I'm preparing to attempt Everest again but, since our trip, Sibu has climbed six of the Seven Summits and, together with Alex Harris, has become part of the first South African team (and first black person) to walk unsupported and unassisted to the South Pole. I certainly don't need to imagine the hardship that feat would have involved, and the determination its success required. But, as you will find, Sibusiso is no stranger to either, and puts his experience with each to good use – not only to overcome physical challenges, but to encourage and motivate others to confront, and perhaps overcome, whatever challenges they may face.

Sir Ranulph Fiennes, March 2008

Acknowledgements

I am deeply humbled to be able to write this story knowing that, without the contributions and support of many great men and women, the story would simply not exist. This book is a product of the efforts of many who had faith, trust and belief in me; they pledged their support and contributed unconditionally. More specifically I will forever feel indebted to:

My lovely and beautiful wife Nomsa for taking my position as head of the family while I am off on my crazy adventures. Darling Nomsa, thank you for your unconditional support always even though you really do not understand why I do these extreme sports. You are the unsung heroine of my success. Thank you for being such a caring and loving person. I really do not know how I would cope without you.

My beautiful children Setsabile, Bhekiwe, Bavukile and Siphosethu. You are a blessing and my pillar of strength at all times. You keep me going when the going gets really tough. Thank you for your support. Having you as my children fills me with joy. You make me feel rich and wealthy.

My friends and supporters, your wishes and prayers give me the strength and the confidence in whatever else I do.

John Doble – you saw a talent lying hidden within me. Thank you for opening my eyes and taking me out of my comfort zone. Your influence in my life has brought about great things for me and my family. From the day that you unleashed the potential in me, you believed in my capabilities, and contributed immensely by supporting me generously without condition. Without your willingness, financial contributions and your time, this story of adventure and achievement wouldn't have come to be. Thank you John, for being a friend who is closer than a brother.

Adam Fleming – you believed in my dream from the very first moment you met me in England. You did not simply believe but you also sponsored me to climb Mount Everest. Very few men in this world are like you. You supported me when I was in need. Thank you so much for your kindness and financial contribution.

Douglas and Penny Watt and Joshua Dlamini, my step-dad, who made a fundamental difference in my life. Thank you for giving me the opportunity to sit in a classroom and learn. You contributed by paying for my school fees but never asked me to pay you back. You taught me a valuable life lesson: to give help without condition. You gave me fatherly love and parental care, you taught me to believe in myself and to always strive to reach new heights. Your support and prayers every day keep me strong. Thank you for forever being my friends.

Bronwyn Roberts, for being such a special friend, and for all that you have done to turn me into professional speaker. Without you this story would still be sitting in my notebooks and my mind. Thank you for believing that my story deserved to be told in a book and for selling my story near and far.

The people and company who paid the salary that supported my family while I was away: Conservation Corporation Africa (CCA). Thank you to the staff at Bongani Mountain Lodge and the staff at Bateleur House (CCA's head office), for your support and respect: Steve Fitzgerald, Nicky Fitzgerald, Shayne Richardson, Hugh Marshall, Julie Moll, Graham, Eric Buthelezi. Thank you for believing in my dream and for affording me the opportunity to climb Mount Everest while my family was looked after by securing my job while I was undertaking my challenge. It is fitting that the second Everest climb benefitted the Africa Foundation, the non-profit organisation in partnership with the CCA that funds and manages projects within communities surrounding CCA conservation areas.

Sir Ranulph Fiennes, you will always be my role model. Thank you for accepting my invitation to climb Mount Everest, and for driving the fundraising, in 2005. I treasure the time we spent together during the expedition. I have fulfilled one of my long-time dreams: to contribute to charity. Thank you so much for inspiring me to do so through our climb.

Thanks are due to the leaders of the first ascent (Steve Bell, Robert Mads Anderson, David Hamilton), for your leadership and guidance, for believing in my abilities and accepting me as one of your clients. The northern side Mount Everest team was phenomenal and the unity and the commitment that you demonstrated while summitting the mountain was awesome. I need to acknowledge specifically the following (in no particular order): Tore Rasmussen, Peggy Foster, Alejandro Garibay, Fred Ziel, Kiek Stam, Ian Parnell, Rodrigo Ponce Limon, Børge Ousland, Jon Gangdal, Tony Wickham, John Crellin and Claire Keeton. And, of course, there are the sherpa teams on both expeditions who worked so hard and yet still somehow remain the unsung heroes. Your willingness to help us succeed certainly paid off for me.

Mark Campbell – you sacrificed the assistance of your climbing sherpa, Mingma, so that he could save my life when I was left for dead in 2005. Mark, you showed me that you value life, and that your victory was not about self. You are a true gentleman. Thank you.

Sherpa Mingma, thank you for saving my life. You lost your chance to summit Everest for the first time in 2005 to help me down to safety. I shall forever be indebted to you.

There is no doubt that this story wouldn't have been turned into a book if it was not for the dedicated hard work and commitment by my co-writer, Gail Jennings, and publisher Tracey Whitelaw of Aardvark Press. Writing this book with you has been another adventure. Thank you for your hospitality, patience and willingness to impart your experience and professionalism in publishing my story.

Achieving dreams like climbing big mountains requires huge financial support. I needed that in 2005 to fulfill my dream of climbing Mount Everest for charity and Anglo American made the finances available for me to attempt the mountain a second time. Anglo American's support meant a great deal to me and to the charities' recipients. Thank for believing in me.

Cape Union Mart made sure that I was looked after very well by providing me with their top range K-Way expedition gear and clothing.

Farouk Abrahams at Batsalani understood my family's needs. Without his support and donation I wouldn't have been able to communicate with my family while I was away climbing the mountain. Your contribution made all the difference in the world.

Kangra Limited and the Graham Beck Foundation's generous contribution benefitted two other charities linked to my second ascent: Birth to Twenty (BT20) and the SOS Children's Village. Your donation has fundamentally changed lives. Thank you very much indeed.

To all those who stretched out a hand and gave to charity as a result of the second climb, thank you very much for supporting a worthy cause.

Prologue

"Where have you climbed before?"
"What's your high-altitude experience?"
"Is this your first time in the Himalayas?"

For the first time since my Everest dream began, I felt horses galloping in my chest ... I was surrounded by thirteen climbers at the Summit Hotel in Kathmandu in October 2002. I was trying to remember their names while at the same time listening to them talk about their long climbing careers.

I, on the other hand, didn't even know the names of some of the equipment I'd brought along, let alone when, why and how I was supposed to use it.

As a game-ranger I had learned a lot about body language ... By looking at an animal, its ears, its tail, the movement of its head, I could usually tell what it was 'thinking', what it was going to do next ... Humans are not that different, and I could tell that I was about to confirm everyone's already sceptical view of me. I plunged into the conversation:

"Yes, it's my first time in the Himalayas. I want to climb Everest in a few months' time, so I thought I would benefit from some high-altitude climbing. Experience? A few 3 000 metre peaks in the Drakensberg that you've probably never have heard of, and Kilimanjaro. Anything above 6 000 metres? Nothing at all!"

I thought it best not to mention that I had only become interested in Everest a few short years before. Until 1998 I had never even seen a photograph of the mountain.

The climbers looked at me as if I was a mad somebody. And I could not blame them. They had only just met me, they did not know me, and they had no idea how far my determination and support had already taken me. And that it would no doubt take me further.

For a few moments, though, my determination wavered. Is this really the right team to be climbing with? My Everest dreams depend on my acceptance by these people, and their judgement of my skills …

I wondered if they doubted me because I was African, because I was black, or merely because I was, after all, very inexperienced.

"Thirty days is nothing," I told myself. "Just stay with them. They know how all this works. You'll learn from them, then leave."

1 Where it all began

Helping a stranger

> I will always love to go to any place you like. Don't hesitate to find out
> from me, if you want to do mountain walks. I promise you that I will
> go with you every time you please.
>
> Sibusiso Vilane to John Doble, 1996

It was the afternoon of a Saturday in 1996 when a tall English man in
his fifties walked up to the front desk of the Malolotja Nature Reserve in
Swaziland. He looked exhausted. I was working at the reserve as a game-
ranger, and was about to go off duty.

The gentleman was checking out after having walked for the better part
of the day. He asked the officer on duty if it was possible to hire guides for
walks in the reserves. I overheard him say that he found the countryside
big and rugged – he felt he might get injured, or lost.

The officer's response was, "No, there are no guides that lead walks here."
But I looked at this man and noticed an individual who was really keen to
walk in the park. I could easily spare a day to help him, I thought.

I gave the man my number, and we made a plan to meet up the following
Saturday.

And that's how I met John Doble.

Sibusiso Vilane had no idea who I was, but said, "I'm not working next Saturday, I'll take you walking."

There was no mention of money, then or afterwards. He gave up his only day off that week to a total stranger, for nothing.

So began a close friendship and my attachment to Swaziland.

John Doble

It turned out that John was the newly-appointed British High Commissioner in Swaziland. He had just arrived in the country, without his family. He had wondered what people did for leisure, so he looked on a map of Swaziland, saw the Reserve and took a drive.

John telephoned me the following Friday to confirm our walk, and the next day we set off. He had forgotten his hiking boots, and had to make do with his fancy, highly-polished work shoes. This did not put him off.

I was to discover, of course, that once John got something into his head, nothing would sway him from his course.

John was determined to reach the second-highest point of the Reserve, at 1 500 metres. It was not an easy walk (especially in fancy shoes). We were often in thick bush, and my companion fell over time and again, getting covered in scratches. I was worried ... I did not want the High Commissioner to come to any harm.

In the end, we achieved our aim; it was the first of many, many targets we set and planned together. Some we reached, some we did not ...

Three weeks later John telephoned and suggested another walk. I helped him climb rocks and difficult ridges, and for some reason he decided that I had a talent as a mountaineer.

And then he mentioned Everest.

"Sibusiso, you climb easily and well," I remember him saying. "I think you would make a good mountaineer, looking at how easily you deal with these rocks.

"The one amazing thing is that no black African has ever climbed Everest," he continued.

Everest? I vaguely remembered hearing about this mountain during my school days, and I hadn't thought about it since.

I wasn't someone who particularly liked walking, as such. I liked the interaction with people during my work as a game-ranger, and I loved the natural environment – it made me feel healthy and alive. I knew which plants you could eat, and how to deal with animals and the weather. I had an understanding of the traditional uses of medicinal plants and I enjoyed being able to share my knowledge of the bush.

But walking? Or mountaineering? I didn't have any gear. We simply used combat boots, and that was about it for equipment. I had not even climbed to the highest point of the Reserve. And I certainly, surely, did not have the time or money to climb Everest.

For John, walking is a serious pastime, and he always refreshes himself afterwards with what seem to be gallons of tea. He also loves horse-riding. He is a history fanatic, and had served in the British Army before he joined the British Foreign Office. His first experience of Africa was of Mozambique, which he loved. John did not enjoy camping at all – he always said he had done enough of that in the army. Once we progressed from day walks, we would be sure to stay in lodges overnight …

After that second walk, we didn't continue with the topic of Everest, but we did begin to climb most of the mountains in Malolotja.

On one of his holidays John invited me to climb in the Drakensberg in South Africa. This was my first experience of this range.

We started with Cathedral Peak (3 004 metres), which required all my physical fitness and endurance. We were down in the late afternoon, to enjoy tea and a delicious dinner at the hotel, where I was the only black customer.

Later I was invited to climb Cleft Peak, Mont-aux-Sources (3 282 metres – the highest peak in South Africa) and Sterkhorn. All the while I was having a lot of fun and starting to develop a real interest in mountaineering.

2 "Get over your fear ..."

Herding cows in Swaziland

Shongwe Mission Hospital, my birthplace, is in what is now Mpumalanga Province, but what was then Kangwane homeland. My mother told me that my birth was in 1970.

When I was about three years old, my traditionally married parents separated. My mother took me and my sister Busisiwe (who was two years younger than me) to live in Swaziland with my father's mother, my grandmother. While we stayed in the Kamavula area, Hhohho Region, my mother left for Mbabane to look for work – she promised to return when she found a place of her own.

My first experience of the outdoor life was as a goat herder for my stepmother's son. Every morning I would take the goats from their night kraal, and drive them to the veld. We had about fifteen animals. I'd stay with them all day, making sure I could see them all the time. At sunset, I'd drive them back home.

Sunset usually meant the end of the day's hardship, as we would have taken nothing with us to eat. I would remember this, decades later, when on the mountain: sunset was a time we feared, for that's when discomfort usually took a turn for the worse.

Breakfast had to sustain us all day: it was a thin porridge with a relish, such as spinach. How I would long for that porridge later, on the big mountain ...

I was too young to count the goats, but lived in fear that I might have lost one or two. I would have been beaten, whipped. This was a bitter time for me: of course I was not paid for my work, and I am still waiting for the goat I was promised.

When I was a little older, perhaps six or seven, my grandmother sent me to work for a nearby family, the Magagulas, as a cattle herder. Some of my contemporaries went to school, but my grandmother did not know the value of education. She had never been educated, and she could not read.

Herding cows is similar to herding goats, but the responsibility is greater. Cows do more damage if they break into someone's crops. Generally, too, I had to walk further to take them to their pastures, sometimes ten kilometres away.

Although I could not yet count, I learned to identify each cow by colour and by shape. Being the youngest cattle herder was not a good experience. The older boys would beat us, ill-treat us, force us to do the hard work while they relaxed. Our elders saw it as a kind of grooming, a way of growing up. That's just what happened.

No one was yet thinking about sending us to school, and I didn't mind. Once, while I was out herding, I walked past a school classroom and saw boys being whipped and caned. For me, schooling looked much worse than cattle herding – more like a slaughterhouse!

Although my mother was not an educated person, she wanted us to be educated. In 1980, when I was about ten, my mother returned from Mbabane, where she had found work as a domestic worker, doing washing and cleaning.

She wanted to take us back with her, but this was not so simple in rural Swaziland. My father didn't want us to go away, so he asked for a debate in front of the chief. My sister and I were asked to make the decision for ourselves.

This was not easy ... but I have a clear memory of my sister and I running after our mother as she caught the bus to the city, us wearing our loinskins and nothing else. It would not be the last time I would find myself looking out of place.

We started in a pre-school at Mahwalala township, where we sang songs, learned poems and played games. My education had commenced and now I desperately wanted it – I could sense that it would be important, essential, in my life.

Soon we made the move, as a family, to a rural area north of Mbabane. Here my mother met Joshua Dlamini, who became our stepfather. What a loving person he was. He treated us as his own children and bought us clothes – including my first pair of shoes. I probably could have been more grateful for those school shoes. I found them difficult and uncomfortable to wear, and used to run home from school with my shoes in my bag. I also found trousers a bit strange, after wearing loinskins ...

Our school was called Zamani Community School. It was a church building made from sticks and mud. It's still there today. One room housed grades 1 and 2, grade 1s facing one direction and grade 2s the other. We would sit on benches and write on our knees. In winter when it was really cold, our teacher would take the board to a nice warm place outside, behind a big rock – and there we used to learn. Our teacher was dedicated to giving us the best education she could. Indeed, you can receive a very good education under a tree – if your teacher is committed.

I passed well, and obtained position one, then topped the class for the whole four years I was there.

In 1984 we moved to a mission school called Mbuluzi Primary. Our house was quite a way away from the school. It was never a simple matter of getting up and going to school – we had an uphill walk for six kilometres – but I liked it, and there was no other way to get about anyway ...

At primary school I discovered soccer and athletics, and I excelled in the 1 500 metre distance and long jump. I became a sports fanatic, and worked hard to develop my physical ability. I represented my school in athletics and soccer, but I never qualified to represent the district or the country. In soccer I played well up front, for I had pace and skill. My mother wouldn't allow me to join an amateur football team. How could I blame her when she did not understand football?

Soon after my arrival at the new school, I was approached by my class teacher, Mrs Masilela, to work for her after lessons. My mother had agreed to this, as she could not afford to give me pocket money.

My first job was to collect firewood for Mrs Masilela's stove. I'd walk the short distance to the gum forest, then collect the wood and chop it. I'd also fetch water for her, and during the ploughing season work in her fields every afternoon, and on Saturdays. Sundays I would be at home.

In 1986 I completed my primary education, obtaining a first class pass with merit (A+), and was admitted to Mater Dolorosa High School in Mbabane. The change from rural to urban school was dramatic. There were two classes per standard and a much further distance to walk each day.

My sister stayed on at the primary school – she had begun to suffer from epilepsy, and this made things very difficult for her.

I did very well during my first year of secondary school, but it was during this year that my schooling almost ended.

I had become used to earning pocket money after working for Mrs Masilela. I would give most of my pay to my mother, but kept a little for myself. Once I started school in the city, I thought that perhaps I should try to find another job.

So it was that during the first long holidays, I started looking for employment. By the time I passed the Watt's house, I was pretty much exhausted. Their gate was wide open – and their garden looked like it needed help. Then I heard the barking of what I was sure were very large dogs, and

I began to back away. "But their garden is overgrown," I said to myself. "Get over your fear of dogs, just go in there and speak to them."

I turned back and stood at the gate as a tiny dog, very fluffy, come darting at me. "There you are," I laughed to myself, "that's what you were afraid of!"

A lady came out of the house, calling her dog, and I presented myself to her. She said that she did not really need a young helper, but she would give me a chance for the day. She ended up giving me a chance for my life.

Her name was Penny, and her husband was Douglas, a geologist who worked for a Canadian company. Her children were Stephen and Kelly.

I worked for the Watts, slashing, clearing and mowing the lawn, and doing other gardening work, every day from nine to three during the school holidays. The hard labour and the walk home was really exhausting! When January came, and with it the school year, I worked on Fridays and Saturdays.

A year later, however, I realised I would have to bid them goodbye. My mother and Mr Dlamini had separated, and my mother would not be able to pay for my schooling. I decided that I would "take the year off" in order to find a better paying job, and save so that I could return to school the following year.

I broke the news to the Watts, and they would have none of it. They would pay for my schooling, they said. They agreed to take me on board, and promised to pay for the rest of my high school. Their offer was so wonderful, so kind, that I did not hesitate to accept the opportunity. I was extremely excited about their promise, and carried on working hard at school, as I was determined to pass.

At the end of 1988 the Watts had to return to Canada, as Douglas's contract had expired. However, they kept their promise to me, and paid my fees until 1991, when I completed my O-levels (with passes in seven out of eight subjects). I wrote to them as often as I could – never thinking that one day I would be in email contact with them, sharing my new challenges and victories.

I think of them often, how they believed in me, and how I nearly lost out on meeting them because of my fear of a dog I hadn't even seen!

Penny Watt: In 1984, my husband Douglas was approached by his company to go with CIDA (Canadian International Development Agency) to a small country in Africa called Swaziland. Our family was excited and unanimously agreed that it was an opportunity that we could not pass up.

During the next two years we prepared to go on an adventure that would expand into a lifetime of hopes and dreams for those we met there. I never expected that someone that we met in Swaziland, whom I look on as an adopted son, would literally reach the top of the world.

When we arrived in Mbabane, we lived in a motel until we were assigned a house on Howe Street. Setting up a home in a different culture to ours in Canada was a challenge. Most of our houseware had to be bought, and the furniture was supplied by the Swazi government. I quickly realised that without the conveniences of my appliances at home, I could not run a household by myself.

We went about hiring someone to keep the house and do laundry (by hand) and another person to keep the garden and grass.

Pauline became our housekeeper and Emmanuel [Sibusiso's English name] became our gardener. Pauline was a mother and a few years older than myself; she had a home of her own. Emmanuel was a schoolboy and roomed in the dorms of the school he was going to. What a blessing they both turned out to be.

Each day that Emmanuel came to do the gardening was a delight. He has the greatest smile and you can see his love of life glinting in his eyes. With only a shovel and a rake, slasher, and a watering hose, he kept the garden and stopped the plant life from entering our front door. I would watch and be amazed as the lawn was being cut by hand and all the other plants and trees were trimmed.

Along with keeping the yard Emmanuel would help with anything we asked of him. Picking avocados was one task. My daughter always received a bump on the head when Doug, my husband, and Emmanuel would drop the avocados to the ground. We had three enormous trees that probably produced a thousand avocados a year. We would give them to people we knew. We ourselves only began eating them during the last year of our time in Swaziland.

Laughter always was a wonderful part of my life in Swaziland and Emmanuel brought with him a love of life that was always filled with laughter. This young boy was only five years older than my son Steven. I was amazed that he had to support himself and help his mother with expenses. To us in Canada this is unheard of. Emmanuel needed support for school fees. In Swaziland the students must pay for all their schooling or they do not get a chance to go to school.

My family stayed in Swaziland for three-and-a-half years and Emmanuel was with us for almost three of them. The time eventually came to return to Canada and it was hard to leave. We had made so many friends and part of our heart will always be in Swaziland.

By now Emmanuel's dreams had become my own, and we tried to help him in any way we could. We made plans to continue his education after we left. In the last weeks we bought school uniforms and went to his school to ensure that he would have a place.

Before we left we promised that if we could, we would return for a visit. With that hope in our heart we left for Canada.

This was just the beginning of our story with Emmanuel. Soon we were receiving letters and his report card for his schooling. The letters were always instantly recognised as Emmanuel's because he would fold them in the most amazing ways. These letters were always a joy to receive.

Emmanuel finished his schooling and, although our financial commitment to him was over, our mutual love for each other continued to grow. Emmanuel has honoured us with the title of parents. His life and dreams are as important to me as my own children's are.

I knew he would go far, but never in my wildest imagination would I think of Emmanuel climbing Mount Everest.

How he got there is his story.

How we helped is a very small part.

3 Game-ranging in Mpumalanga

"If you don't love it, don't do it."

Game-ranging hadn't been my first choice of career after I completed my schooling. But, at that time, 'career' would not have been the right word to use ... I channelled my determination into simply trying to find the work I desperately needed; I was not looking for a career.

In 1992 I left Swaziland to stay with my father and his sister in Jeppes Reef, following a hope that I could register to train as a mechanic at Nkomati Technikon. One of our neighbours in Swaziland had worked as a mechanic – he hadn't even completed high school, but was making good money. This was really what motivated me. (I chose to ignore the fact that my O-levels were not very technical.)

One visit to the Technikon, though, put an end to my dreams of a tertiary education – the fees were so high that there was just no way to afford it.

This turned out to be for the best, as you will see.

My next move was to look for a job, and I found temporary work as a general labourer with self-employed builders in the area. I joined the local soccer team, and made quite a reputation for myself. In fact, I became a household name in our small little neighbourhood and, as I was from Swaziland, I was known as an 'international player'.

Among my fans was a friend who lived a block away from my aunt's house. Sipho had a sister, Nomsa Themba, who attended the nearby high school.

We didn't talk much, but we'd walk home together, and Sipho and Nomsa would cheer for me on the field. I had taken one look at Nomsa and decided that she was a wonderful person. In my culture, you don't first build up a long friendship … You take your chances, and express your feelings as soon as possible. And so I told Nomsa that I would be happy if she became my girlfriend.

At first she didn't buy into the idea.

"I can't be going out with someone who is in everyone's eye," she said. I had to try hard to convince her, and after a few weeks she agreed.

After six months in South Africa, I returned to Swaziland, and found a job once again as a general labourer with a construction company. I remember how we worked in the city centre, surfacing the forecourt of a fuel station. My mother would pass by on a bus, and she would cry as she looked at her boy who had completed his O-levels but was doing pick-and-shovel work. Without a job certificate or any type of qualification, what could I do?

That year-and-a-half of labour taught me the most important lesson about work. "If you don't love it, don't do it!" I made a decision on my first day: "This is not what I want. One must want to get out of bed to do one's work."

I had to stay with what I had, though, while trying to find the right work. Nomsa was pregnant with our first child and she moved to Swaziland to stay with my mother. We knew that as soon as our daughter was born, we needed to have somewhere of our own.

I kept on writing to companies enquiring about jobs, but not one offered even an interview.

While browsing through a telephone book I saw 'Malolotja Nature Reserve'. The name interested me. I didn't know much about the reserve. I had passed it, and had seen the animals. I thought that perhaps game-rangers herded the game, and I knew I could do that. In fact, this appealed to me ...

Despite an initial 'No Job' response, I received a letter from the senior warden two months later, requesting an interview. I took the day off work, arranged for the interview ... and landed a job.

I soon discovered that my duties were varied. The more physically demanding part of the work involved trail clearing and patrolling for poachers along the South African border. I loved the outings in the veld. I received training in rifle handling, as most of the poachers were armed and ready to use their weapons.

The other part of the work was as a tourist officer. I would work at the main gate, sign in the visitors, collect their fee and show them where they could walk or drive.

Some of the rangers said that this type of work was not for educated people. Yes, they considered me, with my O-levels, as educated! I thought they must be mad.

I got stuck in, and grew to really love my job. It was during this time that I began to enjoy views, scenery and walking up mountains – and it was then that I met John.

My salary was a good few hundred more a month than it had been before. Plus, it was a secure job – unlike in the construction industry, I was not so likely to be retrenched.

My next priority was to search for a piece of land on which to build our own home.

Rangers were offered accommodation on the reserve but it was in a tin rondavel, which was rather hot in summer and cold in winter. Families were permitted to stay, but the rondavel was really too small for children.

Nomsa and our first daughter were now staying with her mother in South Africa, and Nomsa was pregnant with our second daughter. I had to find land.

All land in Swaziland is owned by the King, held in trust by him for the Swazi nation. I had the right to live and build a home in the area where I was born, or where my family had been living. There I would have been allocated a land or a house, and fields. However, I'd grown to love the area where Malolotja is situated, the Nkhaba area, which was then under Chief Bhekiphi. And so I had to form an agreement between myself, my mother, Nomsa and the chief's council.

I spoke to a man called Dikida Shabangu, and he represented me when I visited the chief's place to seek land. I would need to explain to the chief, through our mediator, that I would really like to be one of his subjects. If the chief and his council saw me as being a good person, I would be allocated land. I would not have to buy it, but I would be able to live there as long as I liked and my children would be able to inherit.

It was in 1998 that I was eventually allowed permission to build a place of my choice in the area. It is a sparsely-populated area, remote and quiet. Our home would eventually become a little settlement, with the rooms, kitchen and living areas all separate buildings.

I started building slowly, using my time off to cut building poles and material. I was helped by my two brothers-in-law, Sipho Themba and Sifiso Vuma, and we started putting up a four-roomed stick-and-mud house. This required plastering the walls with mud, something that women usually do. Alas, we had to do it ourselves much to the amazement of the neighbours.

In about two weeks we had done a tremendous job, and brought over the roofing material. John was very keen to see me have a house and helped where he could. One Saturday we walked the fifteen kilometres to Lubunyane from Malolotja in order to finish the roof. John hit his finger as he was hammering, and he almost fell from a ladder!

At last, when the house was ready, I fetched Nomsa and our children, so we could all stay at what would now be our first ever permanent home.

4 Climbing Kili

"One step at a time and you surely will reach your destiny."

Well, mountain climbing became possible as a reality to me because
of you.

Sibusiso Vilane to John Doble, 2000

The subject of Everest had again cropped up in conversations with John.
He'd asked around to see if the British army intended any expeditions, but
he received a negative response. As neither of us were climbers, we didn't
know if there were other ways to get to the top.

I had not even seen a photograph of Everest. I hadn't the faintest idea
what it was like. I could not make sense of that kind of height (Everest is
nearly nine kilometres above sea level) but something made me want to
give this mountain a second thought. To be honest, we black Africans generally don't have a sudden urge to climb the mountains in our backyards.
We don't see it as something to be done unless it's an absolute necessity,
or as a job. Mountaineering is simply not a black man's sport. Apart from
anything else, how does one pay for such a trip?

But still, yes, I was driven by a feeling that this is something the world
thinks we can't or won't do. I told John that if I were given the chance to
attempt Everest, I would take it. "I can't promise anything," said John. "But
I will carry on making enquiries."

This was the beginning of a long journey. A journey made shorter by John's persistence, which is like none other.

John started writing letters, and writing more letters, in his tiny, neat handwriting. Not even old-fashioned typing was right for him. He carried on writing letters, from everywhere, to anywhere and anyone, to ensure that together we would climb this mountain. We didn't know it then, but we would climb many mountains to get to the top, and those mountains were not only physical ones.

In 1999 I had the chance to learn whether my dreams of Everest were pure foolishness. After all, if I could not make it to the top of Africa, perhaps I should forget getting to the top of the world.

A Johannesburg-based friend of John's, Mackenzie Rogan, was planning to climb Kilimanjaro. I knew very little about the mountain except that it is the highest in Africa – and that I did not have the money to climb it.

Although John had already climbed Kilimanjaro, he would have loved to do it again. However, the trip was to be in August, two months before John was to retire and leave Swaziland for his home in Devon.

John assured me that money was not an issue, and his friend Mac and his son Rory asked me to join the team.

And so it happened that a few months later, John drove me from Swaziland to Mac's house in Johannesburg, and I met the rest of the team at the airport the following day. Not only was this going to be my first big climb, but it was also my first flight.

Within a matter of hours on the slopes of Kili, I had learned four valuable lessons about myself and climbing.

First: you have to try to climb at your own steady, slow pace. I couldn't understand how the porters could go up so quickly, and some of us young, energetic types made the mistake of trying to follow them. By the time

I reached 3 000 metres (a height I had easily reached in the Drakensberg), I was staggering about, throwing up.

Secondly: that until more black people climb mountains, I'm going to be the odd one out. I felt perfectly at ease with our hiking team, but I did indeed appear strange to the porters. They greeted me in Swahili. They looked at me as if I were a weird person. Eventually the head guide had to explain that I was a paying client, not a wealthy Tanzanian pretending to be a South African …

I felt most uncomfortable being helped by the porters. I never thought anyone would carry my bags for me this way. Some of these guys were my father's age, and they were now serving me. I felt embarrassed that people of his age had to earn a living in the hardest of ways.

The amazing thing was that the porters would wake up early, cook breakfast, then watch us leave. They'd pack up the camp and walk on quickly, passing us along the way, to set up the next camp and cook lunch and dinner. At no stage were we left waiting for anything, and I was stunned by their commitment.

Third: I don't sleep well the higher we climb, and I don't particularly like sharing a tent or a room. This is not to give offence to anyone, but I do like my privacy.

Fourth: that no matter what the conditions or altitude, I always have an appetite! French toast, boiled eggs, chips, chicken, you name it … I love real, good food!

Arriving at last at camp before the summit was exciting indeed, as we knew that that late that evening we would set off for the top. The wake-up call came at 10 pm, and we were required to wear all the warm clothes we had brought.

This was the first time I'd worn long-johns, more than three pairs of socks, and a ski jacket and pants. I looked like a walking wardrobe – I felt like

I was wearing more than I have ever worn in my life, all at once. We used head torches to find the way and ski poles in our hands for support.

After a while I noticed that we were not covering much ground, because of the slow pace we were managing. Ten steps up, then we'd need five to ten minutes to catch our breath. I became uncomfortable with the pace of movement on the mountain. The plan was to stay together and very close. This forced even the quickest and most willing person to walk – and to stop – at the pace of the slowest.

I confronted the team leader and asked to be given my own guide, so that I could walk at a pace that was suitable to me. The leader explained the idea to the whole team. Three others wanted to join me, so we split into two groups.

Perhaps this is another lesson I learned about myself. Am I really a team player? I would need to be, for Everest. Was this something I would have to learn?

The new pace was much more comfortable, as we covered reasonable ground and made good progress. Soon we saw the morning, having climbed throughout the night. We were exhausted but it is as they say: one step at a time and you surely will reach your destiny.

At dawn we were able to see from the landscape below us that we had climbed very high. Then we started encountering snow and ice … We moved on cautiously and, just before sunrise, we saw the summit very close above us. We ambled along … and finally arrived at Uhuru Peak, the top of Africa.

My first thought was relief! And what joy this would give to my friend John. What a moment of brilliance, seeing the sun rise over Africa from the peak. What a beautiful mountain, and how beautiful knowing that this climb could be done.

After taking photographs, we all descended quickly. To be honest, I don't enjoy downhills at all. I find them frustrating. I tend to lose my balance and, on Kili, I almost lost my toenails! What's more, it was rainy, boggy and uncomfortable all the way down – I felt like taking off all my clothes and leaving them there.

Although nothing about my experiences on Kilimanjaro made me think I could not accomplish Everest, The Big One had mostly disappeared from my thinking. I simply did not have the money.

But I had fallen for mountain climbing, and wanted to do more of it. I would have to focus on smaller mountains that I could afford, I thought.

John was all smiles when he met me at Mac's house in Johannesburg. He gave me a hero's welcome.

The following morning we left for Swaziland in John's Landrover, carrying a heavy, steel wagon-wheel, which he wanted to take to his home in Mbabane, and later to Devon. This was not the strangest purchase that John was to drag along with him, as I would discover on a mountain many years later.

5 Survival of the fittest at CCA

"Maybe I can do it with no problem. Who knows?"

Thank you very much for again making enquiries about Everest. Well, to answer your question, I say, yes, I can very much attempt that. Give it a try. But it is as you have said, first things first. Now that I have a home, getting a new job is my primary objective. Then we can plan for Everest. No black person has summitted Everest. But one question comes to my mind: how many black people have been sponsored to try it? Maybe I can do it without any problem. Who knows? But John, please know very well that I want to do it.

Sibusiso Vilane to John Doble, 2000

Nomsa was as pleased as John and I were about my triumph on Kili – and she still talks about climbing the mountain herself with me one day.

John and I had only one outing in Swaziland after this. It was in October 1999, when we decided to camp for the first time at the northern part of Malolotja along the Mgwaniza Mountain Range. We were hoping to get to the top of the highest peak in Swaziland, Bulembu Mountain. As I've mentioned, John doesn't like camping and it's not something I had much experience of, either …

We got to our campsite in time, set up, and set off for a three-hour walk. We had arrived in the late afternoon, just before sunset. Walking at sunset on any mountain is not a good thing, and before long it was dark, and we had lost our way.

We pushed our way through thick bush, and eventually found ourselves among houses in the old asbestos mining town of Bulembu.

We knocked on one of the doors, to ask for help, and it happened to be the home of the mine manager, someone John knew well. We were welcomed inside and offered tea and food. We had landed in good, safe hands.

We left Bulembu around 7 pm, and struggled in the dark without torches. Eventually we got to our site, dug into our sleeping bags and slept without summitting Bulembu Mountain.

Two months later John departed for the UK, but not before I'd found a new position at a different game reserve.

This is Sibusiso once more, our brother. Thank you very much for inviting me and my wife to your farewell party. John, a lot of people gave you a lot of beautiful and exciting, good-looking presents of all sorts. But John, Sibusiso, Nomsa, Setsabile and Bhekiwe had nothing artificial to give you as a gift. All we have is us, but we are giving you us, as a gift. Take us with you everywhere. I am the gift of your spirit and mind. I will be always looking for your reappearance. The family web will not be complete without you, our brother. We will always show that there is one part of us who is not here with us. Have a very good journey. Please be at home eventually. Please rest well and rebuild your house. I will be there in spirit, and wish I could be there helping you too.

Sibusiso Vilane to John Doble, 16 September 1999

For quite some time I had been wanting to get more involved in game-ranging and guiding, and spending more time with tourists. I felt like I was not progressing in my present position – I needed to find another challenge (and a little more money would also have been good).

I had applied to a few game parks, and eventually landed an interview for a selection course at Conservation Corporation Africa (CCA) – thanks to John's contacts. I had my first interview before my trip to Kilimanjaro. Unfortunately I didn't have my driver's licence, though, so this temporarily put an end to those dreams.

I say 'temporarily', as I made sure I got my licence as soon as possible I was tested by one of the country's most feared examiners, someone who'd been trained by the South Africans. I was shaking and shivering with nervousness; I was desperate and only managed to put a smile on my face after I had parked the car at the end of the test. To this day I will never forget how thick the tread on a tyre must be in order for it to be roadworthy. This was the make-or-break question for my test, and I took a good guess. Two millimetres!

I was accepted on the six-week selection course at Phinda. I had saved up all my annual leave and days off, so I would not have to resign first.

I'd say the course was a bit like 'Survivor' – you have to perform all kinds of tasks, exhibit your skills and your capacity for teamwork, and eventually you get selected for the final training – or not.

I learned a great deal during the course, from push-starting cars and camping skills to First Aid, cooking and giving presentations about birds, plants and conservation. I even survived a mind- and body-destroying 35 kilometre hike through the bush carrying sandbags.

Looking back, I'd say that I climbed Everest for the first time then! There was no margin for error, just like it would be on the mountain. In the end, six hopefuls were left of an intake of fourteen. And I was one of them …

6 Failure in the Himalayas?

"Victory never comes free and easy."

I would like to climb Everest, not for myself but for the whole continent of Africa. Even if I make a failed attempt, I'm fine with it – it
would open a new chapter in our history.

Sibusiso Vilane to John Doble, 2002

I chose to work at the CCA lodge closest to my home – Bongani Mountain
Lodge, in Mthethomusha Game Reserve – because I would need to rely on
public transport. Bongani is in South Africa, south of the Kruger National
Park, between Malelane and Nelspruit.

I wasn't doing much hiking or climbing then – after all, my hiking companion, John, had now retired to his farm in Devon. But he had not retired
from letter writing. Oh no ... he had been researching every possible angle
to find out how one actually goes about climbing Everest.

In mid-2002, John wrote to me about Jagged Globe, a mountaineering
company in Sheffield, England. Unlike most other outfits that John had
tried, the manager of Jagged Globe, Steve Bell, actually answered his query.
Bell was married to a woman from Zimbabwe, so perhaps he was interested in an African climber ...

Jagged Globe was keen to consider me as part of their Everest team
in 2003, but first they asked John those revealing questions: "What has

Sibusiso climbed before?" "And what is his high-altitude and extreme weather experience?"

The answers, of course, were nothing and none! Jagged Globe was expecting an answer of at least one other 8 000 metre peak – or at least some 6 000 metre peaks in the Himalayas.

Jagged Globe made it a condition of my acceptance on the team that I gain more experience but, on my budget, I didn't see that as a possibility. They suggested a trip in October 2002 to climb three or four Himalayan peaks over 6 000 metres.

The timing was possible. The trip would take 30 days, and if I accumulated my days off and all my annual leave, I might just make it. I needn't even tell anyone at work where I was going.

That just left the rather large problem of funding.

Everest was not only my dream, but John's, too. So I was not too surprised when he wrote to me again, and said he would pay for me – flights, equipment, expedition fees, hired clothing and even pocket money! This trial climb was my only chance of a ticket into the Everest team.

I have asked John – over and over again – what made him spend this money on me. He had such faith in me, he believed in me, he didn't even think twice before he offered. It is difficult for me to think that I have been taking from people, and not giving, but John has never seen it that way. He says his life would not have been the same had he not met me – and perhaps he is right.

In October 2002 my family and I made our first ever trip to Matsapha International Airport in Swaziland.

It was not easy, as Nomsa was starting to worry. I think she had a glimpse of what the challenges I had set myself really meant.

By now, too, our family had increased. We had welcomed with both hands our new 'bodyguard', Bavukile Birthwell Vilane, our son. His name means 'Risen', the revival of the family. God had answered our prayers well.

And, of course, taking public transport to an airport, and trying to keep to a schedule with a young family in tow, does not make anything easier.

The bus dropped us a few kilometres from the airport, and we were left to walk along towing my bulky expedition bags. Eventually we got a lift in a police van but my biggest worry was how my family was going to get back home. I had given all my money to Nomsa, but still it was not much. Overcoming this anxiety was one of the many metaphorical mountains I climbed in my journey.

As I said goodbye to my family at the airport, it suddenly dawned on me, too, that I might not come back. I watched them leave the airport, trying for a lift to Manzini, then Mbabane. Then as I went into the terminal building, I realised that my family could have stayed to wave me goodbye. I cursed myself. I had had no idea there was a balcony for family and friends to watch the planes land and take off. What a thrill that would have been for my children. And now, what a disappointment.

I called Nomsa from a public phone booth, but they were on their way home in a taxi. I was already missing them, but I focused on our dream. I understood that this dream was part of a bigger picture. I knew it was Africa's dream, too, to show the world how high we can climb!

John met me at the airport in London, from where we travelled to North Wales for what Jagged Globe called a 'pre-expedition weekend'. My climbing team had already attended the training session a month before, but timing and cost had made it impossible for me.

I learned as much as I could about expedition equipment, clothing and tactics. As someone who had seldom camped out before, this was new to me (although I could have done with this knowledge before Kilimanjaro). I call them 'self-management skills' – where to put your socks and underwear in your gear bag so that you don't have to fiddle; how to label your stuff-sacks so you don't waste time and energy searching; why personal hygiene is important so you don't cause others to get sick; and why wet wipes are the answer to almost anything …

John and I hit the road for Sheffield in his classic Morgan convertible. It was a long drive, but I was fascinated to pass cities such as Leeds and Manchester which were familiar to me because of their soccer teams – Lucas Radebe was then with Leeds United.

We arrived in Sheffield in the afternoon, looking forward to our visit to Jagged Globe the next day. Steve Bell himself answered the door. He led us to his office, where we sat down and I started talking about my experience and keenness to climb the queen of the Himalayas.

These were Steve's words of wisdom:

"Everest is a big mountain with many serious accidents. But with experience of being at altitude, good mental preparedness and full dedication to the undertaking, you should be able to do it.

"Learn as much as you can from this trip, ask questions, and you'll gain the experience you need."

Steven's words stuck in my mind when I met up with the rest of the team. Here I have to be honest; I called them my "anti-Everest team". This was my one big chance to get on the Everest team, and my inclusion depended on my experience and their feedback here.

None of my team-mates had Everest on their minds. They were on the trip for its own sake and poured cold water on my dream: it's too dangerous, it's too expensive, do you have any idea what you're up against? They certainly didn't wish me good luck.

I was determined to stick with them, no matter what they thought. I would be able to gain experience with the equipment, find out how my body reacted to extreme conditions and, more than anything, learn to uplift and motivate myself, because no one else was going to do it.

Ed Chad was our expedition leader. An Englishman in his mid-forties, he hadn't climbed Everest but was a high-calibre leader and instructor. He would also be the person to decide my fate, and I would need to impress him if I was to be included on the Everest team.

From Kathmandu, we took a small plane to Lukla (2 600 metres), then trekked toward Namche Bazaar. At the well-known Friendship Hotel, we shared rooms, and this is when I realised that money makes your life there. Water, tea, food, showers – you have to pay for each of them, between 150 and 200 rupees.

I was already being affected by the altitude – I had a headache that was so bad that my skin was sore. Ed gave me the best advice – keep drinking water.

It was here that I realised I was not equipped with good clothes. I had no thick fleece jacket, and no fleece pants and I became really cold. These items had been on my kit list, but I didn't know what they were, so I just didn't get them. John and I had tried to play the game economically – technical gear is very expensive and we only picked up what we thought was vital. So there I was, in my T-shirts and CCA fleece top which was made for the not-very-cold climate of Nelspruit …

We had had the foresight (or was it beginner's luck?) to hire a down jacket, and this was my lifesaver. I started wearing it in Lukla, much to the astonishment of my team-mates. "If you're cold here, you'll die on Everest," they said. Little did they know that I had nothing but a T-shirt on underneath.

It was also in Lukla that I first encountered Nepalese food: rice, vegetables and dhal. I fell in love with dhal, and thought that I might have to break away from the rest of the group and eat dhal with the sherpas during the climb.

In my view, trekking is just hiking – for some reason people seem to want to give it a fancy name. And it's funny that this fancy name comes from Afrikaans.

Generally the trekking route was easy, even though I was feeling head-achy. As we hit the 3 200 metres above sea level mark, we found a stunning view of the man-eating monster mountain, the queen herself. Everest looked scary big!

By the time we reached an altitude of 5 145 metres, I found it difficult to sleep – my hammering headaches made each night excruciatingly long. The skin on my forehead was painful, so I was drinking four to five litres of water a day to try and assuage the pain.

Then there was the business of getting out of bed at night to pee. I hadn't taken to the idea of a pee bottle – as an African man, I was just not going to do it. So soon I started cheating on the drinking – nothing after lunch – but then I became even more sick ... Eventually I scouted for a pee bottle, but I had no money to spare to buy one!

Our first summit of the trip was to be Pokhalde – it is a bit higher than Kili at about 5 900 metres.

We were given a wake-up call at 5 am. We dressed quickly, and forced down our breakfast of dumplings, beans, curries and rice pudding.

I was roped up to Ed Chad and two other climbers. There was fair bit of rock scrambling, then a section of snow, which required crampons. This was no pleasant climb for me. I was very cold; my hands were freezing. I realised that when it came to the Big One, I'd need to invest in better gear.

Eventually, though, I did get to squeeze in among the other team members to stand at the summit, which is so small that standing up and moving freely is not really possible. We looked around in jubilation and enjoyed the views of the other peaks. Then we started down the mountain.

I almost fainted when I saw the other members going down backwards, hanging on the ropes on their figure of eights and abseiling along the fixed ropes. Slowly but surely I tried, and was amazed how great I felt when I got down. I felt good, like a champion, and it was at this moment that my confidence started building. I learned that by being totally committed, almost any goal is possible.

My understanding of the equipment was also getting better. After our triumph at Pokhalde I was beginning to feel at ease, but still I chose to sleep alone in a tent that night, rather than share a room in the tea house.

Our next summit was to be Island Peak, which stands at 6 189 metres. I really enjoyed this climb. We started by rock scrambling for about an hour before hitting some snow patches. By now I liked using crampons as they really made me feel comfortable; without them, I looked like a newly-born giraffe trying to walk.

The summit of Island Peak is heaven. All the team members got to the top and, as I stood there, I saw Everest in my grasp. Standing on this second summit, I knew there was indeed a chance for me to qualify for the Everest team.

The descent was not at all amusing – it was just too long. I was now also missing my family, and had thought about them throughout the night. The only time I'd spent this long without them before (three weeks) was when I was doing the ranger course at Phinda, and then I was near a telephone.

Dreams can become a reality, provided you have a great team that is sharing the same goal.

It was after Island Peak, at Dinboche Lodge, that I started to see Everest slip from my grasp. My vision of Everest success while standing at the summit of Island Peak had been all too fleeting.

We celebrated our summit by sleeping under a roof, with hot lemon tea, and dinner around a yak-dung fire. But it was too good, too comfortable, and the rest of the team wanted to stay there for one more day.

This was the summit of their dream, but only a stepping stone for mine.

If we stayed here for this extra day, we might not make all the planned summits, and I might not satisfy the requirements for the Everest team …

I didn't voice my concerns. My inexperience put me at the bottom of the hierarchy – at least that's how I felt. I felt watched. Was my conduct and teamwork being judged as acceptable? So it was the 'silence is golden' game for me. After our unexpected rest day, we were off again, aiming for the peak of Lobuje East. I decided to dedicate this climb to my son Bavukile, who was then five months old.

One of our team members had been nursing a persistent cough. It happened to worsen at this juncture, and he realised that he would not have a good climb. It was at this point that the unexpected happened yet again. The leader of the expedition decided to turn back with him, to ensure that he returned safely. We continued with the sherpas, and made positive progress up the peak. I was on top of my game here, leading the pack for quite some time.

We took a few steps up on the rope, and then a large amount of time catching our breath. What an experience. Our 'chain' would cover a few hundred metres.

When we were just two or so hours from the summit, we saw a team of climbers on their way down. We greeted them as they passed – we were so close, I knew we could make it.

Suddenly I heard a whistle from below. I stopped instantly. One of the guys going down had fallen over the edge.

I was shocked, and couldn't say anything for a while. All I could think of was how this could be possible. I asked our *sirdar* what we should do – how could we help?

"We cannot help for he is as good as dead where he has fallen," he said, and indeed he was right.

One of our team was by now shaking with terror. We discussed our next move – should we continue?

Of course I wanted to pursue the summit – and one other climber, together with the sherpas, agreed. But, as a team, we started to lose our focus. The others wanted to turn back, traumatised by the death of the climber, they said, and fearing that our slow progress, our waiting at the ropes for everyone to catch up, and our debating about our progress, had set us back too much timewise.

I saw this as defeat, brought on by shock and fatigue – and the fact was that our team leader was not with us to make the right choice.

Turning back was a painful decision, but I did it, for we were doing everything as a team. I was sobbing inside – was this my chance at Everest blown?

When we reached camp, I went straight to my tent. I didn't want to talk to anyone. Ed Chad noticed that I was angry about something, so he called a meeting and we discussed the day. Nothing could be done – I would be going home disappointed.

And worse. Ed made the decision that we would end our Himalayan expedition here – we had run out of time, and inclination, to attempt that fourth summit, Pharchemuche. Instead, we could take a leisurely hike to recover.

I felt cold. I hated this moment so much that I didn't said a word.

It was, of course, one of those lessons in teamwork: stay together even if all is not working in your favour, and you have to rely on another person's decision.

From that moment on I simply followed the majority. Who was I to blow against the wind? This is what I whispered to myself.

Our hike was to a place called Gokyo, over the Chola Pass. I had been dragging my feet, feeling unmotivated and miserable, until we passed a set of frozen lakes.

They were incredible – where in Africa would I have seen anything like this? We threw stones – rocks, even – into the pools, and they just rested on the surface. To be honest, though, I would not chance a walk on the lake – I was certain I'd sink and drown.

I picked up my pace and gave myself some distance between myself and the other guys; I wanted to enjoy the stillness and think of my family.

I found a piece of bamboo, which was about half a metre long, and used it carve the names of my family in the snow. I included John and his daughter, Louisa. I suddenly felt encouraged, and there was a brightness again in my mind.

The next day I walked up to the summit of the Gokyo Ree – and once again caught a glimpse of my dream summit. I will get there, I told myself.

7 Another step closer to Everest

"Some people have heart."

I thought that my place on the Everest team was dependent on one man, Ed Chad but, as usual, it was dependent on John.

Back in the UK, John and I discussed my experiences, then we telephoned Steve Bell. He was thrilled to hear my excitement, but noted that he could not guarantee anything; he was waiting for an official report about my abilities. I hoped for the best, but feared the worst.

I felt that twinge of doubt, as I knew Ed wouldn't favour me after the Lobuje saga.

I had been angry, had kept to myself, and didn't participate much after the third summit was terminated. I'd stopped short of being rude, but my unhappiness must have cast a shadow.

So I returned to my beloved family and work at Bongani Mountain Lodge. From there, I waited patiently for John to tell about my chances.

In November that year (2002), John told me that he was conducting his next letter-writing campaign – to find me a sponsor. "Relax, settle down and make your mind ready," he said.

What he didn't tell me – at least, not then – was that he was conducting two letter-writing campaigns. Letter after letter, and telephone call after telephone call, he was in contact with Jagged Globe.

Neither of us ever got to read Ed's report, but John got to hear the short summary: "No".

He asked to hear the longer version: "No, we think that it would not be right to have Sibusiso on the team. He is not a team player. He's also not experienced enough. He's not ready."

It was suggested that if I was still keen, I should start on a four-year training programme, including a trip to Equador that December.

Yet John had faith. He wanted to see our Everest trip happen, and he knew that the criticism of me was not true. (Well, put it this way, he knew that maybe some of it was true, but he also knew I'd have improved my teamwork and climbing skills by the time we reached the Himalayas again.)

To my mind then, all that was between me and Everest was the funding. John assured me he was working on it, and I started training: running, aerobics, stretching and soccer. Three fellow rangers joined in – Gideon, Meshak and Sifiso – spurred on by the desire not to be outwalked by their clients in the reserve. They really motivated me, even though they did not understand my need to climb. Running in the Reserve wasn't easy – I couldn't run very far before I had to turn back to the safety of the main camp. After all, there were lions about!

People would ask me how I was preparing myself mentally for the challenge. At first I battled to answer. There were times where I responded that I was doing nothing. That is when they would say that climbing Everest is all in the brain, and that should be my primary training.

I certainly agreed there, but I suppose that 'thinking positively' about the mountain had by now become second nature.

I also tried to read stories about Everest expeditions. I read Jon Krakauer's *Into Thin Air* in one sitting, digesting everything. I imagined the mountain and me climbing, passing the places where people had fallen and died. But I never imagined myself falling, or even turning back. I visualised myself climbing surely on very steep snow and ice, and getting to the top.

By the end of November, John had persuaded the Jagged Globe team to accepted me on the 2003 expedition team, just four months away. There was one more condition – I had to attend a one-week winter mountaineering course in Scotland, just before the expedition. Steve Bell had written that, "Sibusiso has to camp for one night on Ben Nevis, as this will give him a clue as to what to expect on Everest under extremes."

I welcomed this condition – all the better for me to get to the top.

John was so willing to see this dream materialise that he was going to pay for the course in Scotland as well as Everest, using money he'd set aside to buy a racehorse.

I did not like the fact that John would be footing the cost. I knew that he had done so much for me already, and I was now aware that we needed about 60 000 US dollars.

In October, when John and I had travelled briefly in England before my trip to the Himalayas, we'd stopped in to visit friends – a couple he'd met in Johannesburg years earlier. John had mentioned our Everest dream, and his friend, who was on the board of one of South Africa's biggest mining houses, had promised to try to secure funding for me. Much as he and John tried, however, no corporates or foundations saw my trip as something they saw fit to sponsor.

December rolled by, and 14 March 2003, the date on which I was to leave, was looming.

In the end, John didn't have to spend his own money. He didn't buy a race-horse, either – instead he bought himself a place on the mountaineering skills course in Scotland, and a trip to Everest Base Camp to meet me.

That's because the very same gentleman who was searching for sponsorship decided to sponsor me himself. He asked for his name to be kept out of the media at the time but my benefactor was Adam Fleming.

Adam wrote to me to tell me of his gift. "I can't think of any money better spent," he said. Before John and I left for the Himalayas, the three of us enjoyed a dinner together. "Don't think of the money we have paid for you," they said. "It does not matter. We are helping you as a friend. We don't want you to force yourself just because we have put money on your shoulder. All that is important is that you come back alive."

These were very empowering words. Some people have heart. They don't want you to prove your capabilities before they help you. They look at you and want to help you without conditions ...

If this world was full of people like that, a lot of hidden talent would be discovered.

I knew that I was heading for the unknown, and that it might cost me my life. Nomsa was, as usual, full of encouragement and courage – she knew I was doing this for my family.

March 13 was, not surprisingly, a busy day. But in the afternoon of this last day with my family, while I was frantically packing, we were visited by a BBC crew. They had heard about me from John's friends in South Africa. In an interview with Nomsa, she said that, yes, she was scared, but that she obviously hoped I would go and climb successfully. I felt very tense leaving my family that day. We prayed and I couldn't hold myself back; for the first time I wept in front of my kids.

The BBC crew filmed my departure – by bus – to the capital Mbabane, from where I hired a taxi to the airport.

John's friends had organised another 'surprise' for me – at Johannesburg airport I was called to the VIP lounge. Waiting for me there was the then-South African minister of environmental affairs and tourism, Mr Valli Moosa.

The minister was sipping a cup of coffee when I walked in, and immediately he stood up and greeted me. "I thought I was going to see a giant," he said, "but you are not one!"

He handed me a South African flag, which I accepted with pride. "Please put this on top of Everest for us," he said.

If you asked me to describe the scenery along the road from Heathrow to Scotland, I'd give you a blank stare – despite the sunny skies and the fact that John had put down the roof of the Morgan. That's because John and I talked non-stop throughout the trip, and because once my mind is focused on something, it stays focused. Scotland was where I'd do my last round of training, so Scotland was where I was focused, not on the route there!

John had enrolled on the introductory climbing course, and his fumbling with the gear and big plastic boots reminded me of my learning experiences only a few months back.

The course turned out to be worth every moment. We learned about walking on snow, dealing with accidents, how to identify hazards such as crevasses and cornices, and how to deal with avalanches. I paid attention.

One evening at our hotel I received a telephone call from Rebecca Stephens who, in 1993, became the first British woman to climb Everest. She had heard about me from John, who had attended one of her talks. I was honoured to speak to Rebecca, as I was just about to start reading her memoir, *On Top of the World*.

She advised me to respect the mountains, drink lots of liquids, and never to compete with anyone while climbing. I have remembered her advice ever since.

Ben Nevis was our goal. On the appointed day we were lucky that the weather stayed clear. The talk was that this was unusual in Scotland in March. I thought to myself that there was an African there, so the sky should be African and warm.

Our overnight rations were boil-in-the-bag dumplings, rice pudding and curry. Oh no, I thought, I don't like rice pudding at all. And I don't really like curry, either … On Kilimanjaro, the food was always freshly prepared; on this type of climb, we would end up with mostly pre-cooked, dehydrated food.

I slept very well that night. I was feeling very motivated and knew that seeing the summit of Everest was now entirely possible. I realised that my support came from a long way, not only from Africa.

Steve Bell had wanted me to camp in extreme weather overnight to see how frightened and cold I would be. Maybe I would decide to quit ... Ben Nevis was certainly colder than the lower Himalayas, but I had experienced worse, and it is not like me to give up. I knew very well that victory never comes easily.

The place where we pitched our tent that night was exposed, open to the wind and cold. The views were amazing toward sunset, and I strolled about, taking pictures.

We settled and realised that the wind was picking up. I had to build a snow wall about a metre high around the tent to serve as a windbreak. I never thought that snow would be so difficult and impossible to dig. After a few attempts I was sweating.

There is a lot that you learn when you camp out in the cold, sharing a tent with a woman. With limited room you have to organise yourselves well! We had great fun as my guide, Adele, kept offering tips about how to work together and be aware of each other's personal space: divide your space with your expedition bag, she suggested, cook at the entrance of the tent, clean your boots and shoes before walking inside, sleep with your boot inners still on ... all the things that many people might take for granted. And, of course, never ever wear your crampons inside!

A BBC film crew was there to meet me at the end of the course. I was asked the familiar question: why? I gave them my usual answer: "I want to show the world that Africans can do it too."

8 Base Camp and beyond

"When thinking positively becomes second nature."

Penny Watt: When Emmanuel wrote that he was going to climb Everest, I was stunned. A boy who started life with nothing was aiming for the top of the world. The pride we always had in Emmanuel is growing. I was also concerned with him taking on such an enormous undertaking.

I remember telling him that the God who made Everest was the only One who could bring him home safely. I asked him to remember to pray each time he took a step. I realised every step held an element of danger and knew Our Lord had Emmanuel in His hands.

The story continues. The mountains are not Emmanuel's only goals. I see a young man striving to help others wherever he can. I have an adopted son whose goals are beyond what I can ever imagine.

When I was asked to write my memories about Emmanuel I was taken by surprise. I had little input to his life and that he valued this input so much is a great honour. We gave a little to Africa. Africa has given us much. The Lord truly guides our going and our coming in. He will do the same for Emmanuel.

Sunday 23 March: the day had arrived! John and I went to his local church, and the pastor prayed that I would have a safe and successful climb. I was quietly confident, and believed that the Lord was indeed going to guide me safely.

When John bid me farewell at the airport, I felt as though a part of me was missing. Steve Bell and I travelled together from there and we were to meet the rest of the team at Kathmandu.

Kiek Stam, one of our team, would become like a father to me on that trip. A former CEO of Philips in the Netherlands, he would go on to climb all seven summits. A good and willing person, he would take a great deal of trouble to get to know me and take an interest in me.

David Hamilton was to assist the leader of the expedition, Robert Mads Anderson.

Our first night was in the Summit Hotel, from where we would trek for ten days to Base Camp, staying in tea houses along the way. We would be doing enough camping later! We were in no rush – we'd be spending at least 77 days on the mountain. We might as well get on and enjoy the trek.

The tea house accommodation was warm and, of course, we would be sleeping on beds. The other good thing was that we could decide what we wanted to eat – and it wasn't the same every day. Vegetable rice, fried noodles … and lots of tea.

I made the most of the available choices, as I knew that as soon as we were on the mountain, we would be eating expedition food and then there would be no point craving different foods, or imagining what I'd rather be eating. I suspected that it would not be a good idea to lose focus and think about scrambled eggs instead. Although my staple at home is pap – Nomsa makes it very well – I am not someone who can't go for a day without pap and meat. Most Africans I know would not be able to cope with rice and dhal day in and day out, but I adapted. To be honest, though, those rice puddings and dumplings were eaten out of desperation and I wouldn't have minded a pizza or two along the way.

I was amazed to find that I had not yet suffered from a headache. This was the opposite of my experience of the Himalayas in October 2002, when I was cursing the gods as terrible explosions in my head kept me awake.

As we passed sherpa villages, the young children would turn and stare at me. By their body language I knew they were talking about me … I so wished I could ask them what they were thinking.

At Namche Bazaar I shared a tent with Kiek, who noticed that I did not have a reading torch, or lightweight shoes. The following day he came to me with a pair of sandals and a reading lamp – he took so much trouble to make me feel welcome, without being patronising. This was indeed the beginning of a real friendship.

At Everest View Hotel, I saw Everest again, with a cloud veiling her summit. The mountains never spoke loudly, but silently, and to me Everest said: "Sibusiso, you are welcome to stand at the top."

It was great for me to be here again – it was familiar country although this time everything was covered in snow. My diary entry read: "How lucky I am to be here doing this, thanks to God and to John."

My first glimpse of Base Camp was a motivating one. We spent two hours walking there from our tea house. All the while we were accompanied by the ringing of the yak bells on the beasts also heading up the mountain. Base Camp looked busier and busier as we got closer. There were already many tents, signalling that there were plenty of people and teams gearing up for the challenge. I saw American, British, French, German and Canadian flags. I also spotted my own country's flag, flown by the South African Discovery Team.

The Khumbu Icefall came into sight clearly for the first time, and I scrutinised the passage to the top of the world above it. I thought of my family and how lucky, proud and fortunate I was to be at this point, and how important it was for myself, my family, tribe and country.

We chose a secluded spot, right near the edge of the camp and protected from the wind. We would not share tents here, but would meet up at the mess tent. Along with the mess tent, there were communication tents, cooks' tents and a storeroom tent, with all our food supplies. Some of the sherpas had not seen a black man before. Every time I looked in their direction, they would look away, but at times they would smile at me. I was keen to speak to them, and so I made friends with a few within the first week of my being at Base Camp.

The goal of the first quarter of any Everest climb is acclimatisation, so we took things easy.

Our daily routine would start with tea in bed served by the kitchen team, then a hasty wash in five litres of water (in a bowl). Hot showers were also available – as an alternative to those five litres. From about 8 am every morning we'd gather in the mess tent, chat for a while, and then retire to our tents to read or sleep. When I got up it was usually about lunchtime, and I'd take my book and head to the mess tent for food and reading.

I was resting well and feeling strong, but I was missing my family. The evenings were quiet and the cold became almost unbearable. After sunset the temperature would also settle at between –15 to –20 °C, not favourable for a man from Africa – and Nelspruit in particular.

Other team members started to move around Base Camp, visiting one another. Because of the attention I was attracting wherever I went, I chose to keep to myself for a while but it was not long before the South African team – sponsored by Discovery Health – learned of my presence, and showed up at our camp one afternoon.

The team leader was Alex Harris, and he visited along with two Shauns and a Laurence. It was great to meet my compatriots but I sensed that they thought I might be there in 'competition' to them. After all, theirs was the first purely South African team aiming for the top. I explained that I was born South African but grew up in Swaziland, and that I was not a mountaineer but a game-ranger with my own particular motivation for getting to the top. That seemed to reassure them.

Puja Day on 6 April was a big day for everyone at Jagged Globe's camp, as we were to be blessed by the *lama*. I had already been prayed for by the pastor of John's church – and many others – but I wasn't going to turn away additional blessings.

The sherpas don't move much beyond Base Camp before Puja Day. A ceremony conducted by a local *lama* who prays for safety and success on the mountain.

We placed our climbing equipment under the *stupa*, a Buddhist ceremonial altar-like structure), which was decorated with strings of prayer flags. We were offered juice and a fermented rice drink called *chang*. While the *lama* was chanting, each climber was given a red string to weave around his neck for good luck, and rice to throw in all directions.

While we hesitantly sipped our *chang*, the sherpas really dug into the stuff. This was to be their last beer for two months or so, so they set out to enjoy it to the fullest.

I felt so close to God on this day, and I felt confident that the Lord would lead me safely to the very top of the world.

It was 7 April and time to start moving. Climbing Everest is a tedious process. The acclimatisation routine is the same for all teams: climb to Camp One (6 000 metres), stay overnight, rest, move on to Camp Two (6 200 metres). Stay one or two nights, then back to Base Camp (5 300 metres) … And then we'd do it all over again, moving higher and higher, then back down again.

There's a permanent cook at Base Camp and at Camp Two, and between these camps, it's expedition food … The expedition food is OK for the first week, but by day 60, it gets difficult to stomach. There are energy bars, chocolate bars and sweets, but I don't really like sweet things, so I found myself battling a bit.

Three to four weeks into the acclimatisation programme, we were comfortable at Camp Three (7 300 metres).

Then we would be subject to the waiting game.

9 A new personal record

"My highest altitude ever – for now."

On the morning we first left for Camp One (9 April), I battled to get everything right. Although I'd learned, in theory and a bit of practice, how to wear a climbing harness, it just didn't come naturally to me.

I forced down some porridge and a cup of tea, then we walked slowly out on to the moraine to the accompaniment of much swearing as we tripped on everyone else's guy ropes.

Once we hit the boulders at the start of the Khumbu Icefall, we needed our crampons, and slowly, slowly we clipped into the fixed ropes and moved up with caution. The sun hit the icefall at about 9 am, and we enjoyed lovely views. Dangerous as it is, the icefall is really very beautiful and you can never take enough photographs. We made our way down again, had lunch at Camp One, and then returned to Base Camp.

Three days we started the serious business. We split into two groups: one led by David Hamilton and the other by Robert Anderson. As planned, we got a wake-up call at 2.30 am. It took me over half an hour to be fully dressed and ready – I'm really not one for early mornings.

This was the most anticipated move, as it would allow us to gauge our strength and how well we were acclimatising. Slowly we gained some ground, and although I was not moving as quickly as some of the other team members, I did not mind. What I did mind, though, was that my fingers were getting very, very cold: I was wearing a pair of thin gloves and mittens that John had lent me. I was unable to use my hands, and had made the mistake of packing my good gloves right at the bottom of my rucksack. This is something mountaineers never want to do.

We stopped for a short time to rest and then I munched a biscuit as we slowly continued up the snow ridges. Finally I saw tents a few paces away as we arrived, exhausted, at Camp One

I devoured my lunch: boil-in-the-bag chicken dumplings, and loads of tea. Until I met John, I would only ever drink tea in the morning, with my bread. In my culture, you would never just 'have a cup of tea'. But after walking with John, I had become accustomed to drinking tea and eating biscuits. I discovered that tea was a marvellous way of quenching my thirst. I also found the ritual relaxing. Here, on Everest, our drinking water was so cold that tea was even more welcome, and I filled my bottle with black tea.

After a night of disturbed sleep – I had a pounding headache – we started for Base Camp again where I spent a good few hours putting pen to paper, writing to my wife and to John. Most of the others were emailing friends and families, but back then I didn't know how to use a computer …

It would be three days before we'd contemplate moving up the mountain again. There's lots of boredom on these expeditions. On a rest day you do absolutely nothing; you get up and have your morning meal, then the day lays out before you.

Card games were popular among the teams, but I didn't know how to play any of the games they played, such as bridge. I had three good books to keep me going, though: the Bible that the Watts had given me, *On Top of the World* by Rebecca Stephens and Jamling Tenzing Norgay's book, *Touching My Father's Soul: A Sherpa's Journey to the Top of Everest*.

When I was feeling lonely, the boredom didn't help. That's the mind challenge, of course. However, I never started to think that the expedition was a waste of time. It never got to me; I never thought, "Why I am torturing myself?" I simply kept telling myself, "Be patient. Just go and do it".

On our next trip up to Camp One (16 April), I woke up late at 2.30 am, and by the time I got outside to fill my water bottle, everybody was ready to leave. I feared that this was going to be my pattern. I was already in a rush, but soon the rest of the team was advancing towards the Khumbu Icefall. I tried to pick up my pace, but began coughing and puffing along in a state of panic. I decided to stop rushing, and it worked for me – I recovered slowly and regained some strength.

The icefall was soon ablaze with headlamps connecting and following each other, sometimes in zigzags up the fall towards Camp One.

We all took it easy once we started climbing the icefall. This place is never a joke. You never get used to the terrain, no matter how many times you go up and down this section.

It felt good to be back at Camp One. There is not much activity at these high camps, so we each hibernated in our tents and made food: boil-in-the-bag brew again – mashed potatoes, rice pudding and dumplings.

I was still motivated and my health was excellent. The next morning we headed along the vast snowfield called the Western Cwm. This place appears to go on forever. We crossed several hundred crevasses using the fixed and anchored aluminium ladders. A few times we powered up steep ridges that needed climbing jumars.

After a gruelling seven hours we reached Camp Two. I'd reached my highest altitude ever at 6 200 metres.

I was also delighted because there was a permanent cook there. We were welcomed with lemon tea, which went down very well. We were to share tents here, but luckily for me, since I was the shortest and smallest, I was given one of the very small, 'unsharable' tents.

I spent two days by myself, reading or lying in my sleeping bag. I still felt a little uncomfortable being the only black person on the mountain. I didn't like visiting the other camps in case I was confronted by that familiar question-mark-look on people's faces.

I had always realised that Everest was going to be a tough climb, and now I was feeling the reality. Our next climb was to the foot of the Lhotse Face, just above the Cwm but below Camp Three. While some of our team climbed 100 metres further up the face, I was crippled by exhaustion only 30 metres up. Lhotse is daunting: blue ice, very slippery, but spectacular. And depending on the team's acclimatisation, we might have to climb up – and down – this face a number of times.

We went down to Base Camp in heavy snow – with the thought of a hot shower keeping me going. I already felt as if I had accomplished my dream, yet in truth I was still very far from realising it. Nevertheless, it was motivating to have come this far already.

We needed the rest and stamina-building back at Base Camp, with three days of snoozing, doing our laundry and reading/eating/card games before heading for the high camps again.

Then acclimatisation started again: up at 1.30 am, breakfast of baked beans and toast at 2 am, on the ice by 3 am. And so it was that on 23 April we watched the moon rise over the Khumbu Icefall, and then we passed Camp One … It was heaven on earth, if it were not for the dangers of being here.

Eight hours later I was at Camp Two. I felt like I was suffering from heat stroke. I had started taking off my layers of clothing, and am fortunate indeed that my skin does not burn. While my team mates were becoming unidentifiable, with cracking lips and flaking skin, my skin wasn't too badly affected – except for frost-nip on my fingers.

At camp all we did was sleep, and pack up a few necessities for the high camp. I was beginning to worry about Camp Three and beyond. At 7 200 metres and on the worst face, the climb would be steep and dangerous. But if I got to Three, I would once again have set my own personal record.

10 A hard day's walk

"There are no short cuts to the top of the world."

Our journey to Camp Three from Camp Two was quick and, unsurprisingly, accompanied by spectacular views. Before midday I was standing at a record (for me) 7 200 metres above sea level.

I had gained a great deal of experience using ropes and crampons during this climb. I was jubilant when I got in to camp because it was mission-accomplished in terms of our team's acclimatisation plans. We all knew that after this came the 'death zone'.

The weather was not too bad, but a little windy. The slope made movement limited, and the tents were squeezed together. Sharing was something of a nightmare, as a two-person tent hardly slept two people, let alone enabled us to prepare our meals as well. I was sharing with Kiek, who is a big man; I woke up a couple of times because he seemed to have mistaken me for a mattress.

The views from Camp Three were lovely, especially from the door of the tent in the direction of the Western Cwm. Then the wind picked up, and it felt as if we might be buried in an avalanche any minute. I was relieved when I put on my rucksack and clipped on to the rope for the trip down again.

All this up-and-down is surprising for people who don't climb, but the lesson is that there are literally no short cuts to the top of the world. Cheat

Sibusiso on Khumbu Icefall towards Western Cwm, south side

Climbers on Khumbu Icefall before camp on the Western Cwm, south side

Crossing the notoriously dangerous Khumbu Icefall, south side

Camp Two below Lhotse Face, south side

Steep ice on Lhotse Face, south side

Camp Three on Lhotse Face, south side

Lhotse Face above Camp Three, south side

Traffic on Lhotse Face above Camp Three, south side

©Børge Ousland

Hard work on Lhotse Face, south side

©Børge Ousland

A view of the south summit, from below Hillary Step

©David Hamilton

Sibusiso and Robert Anderson on top of the world, south summit 2003

©Ian Parnell

Ran Fiennes and Sibusiso passing seracs as they head to Advance Base Camp, north side

Ran Fiennes and Sibusiso at Advance Base Camp, north side

©Ian Parnell

Fresh snow covers tents at Camp One, north side

Above North Col (Camp One), north side

©Sibusiso Vilane

©Sibusiso Vilane

on the route, and you might never get there. It requires all your effort, patience and focus.

Back at the Base Camp once again, we rested for a few days before discussing our summit bid. We were then subjected to a period of frustration, which we called the 'waiting game'.

We sat at Base Camp for a week, and the weather was terrible. We were all waiting for the weather window of opportunity that would allow us an attempt on the summit. But day in, day out, the bad weather continued. An uncompromising cloud appeared to be blowing in a whirlwind just from the top of Everest.

I had the opportunity to telephone home via satellite phone. Except for letters and postcards those five weeks, I had had no communication with my family (and some of the letters only arrived three months after my return). Without the kindness of Kiek, who paid for the call, I would never have been able to hear their voices this far away from home.

Nomsa was surprised, and excited, to hear from me. But, although she tried to assure me that all was fine at home, I knew from the tone of her voice that things were not going well. She reluctantly broke the news that one of our houses, our traditional cooking hut, had been set alight by vandals early one morning. Our stick-and-mud house nearby had not been affected because it had a corrugated iron roof and our neighbours had immediately come to help. Everything that was inside the thatched hut was destroyed in the fire.

There I was, on Everest, with strong winds howling, and I had no idea when I would return. I imagined my family, my son only fifteen months old, and my wife, Nomsa, going through all this without me, with no one to call. It was frightening. I knew, though, that it would be a double loss to my family if I were to leave the expedition. I knew that my victory would bring them joy.

After I said goodbye to Nomsa, I told Kiek what had happened, and went to my tent. I could not contain myself. I prayed and wept and debated the motive behind the arson. But I heard a voice in my mind: "Don't worry so much, and be happy and grateful that your family is still alive and nobody has been injured. Don't give up on the climb, and get to the top, for that will bring a smile to your family."

I wiped my eyes and crawled out of my tent to meet everybody at the mess tent. Kiek had already briefed them about my family's ordeal, but I explained that I would be staying until the expedition was complete. It was hard not to think of the why and by whom, but I decided that I would not allow distant enemies to disturb our dream.

In fact, the 'waiting game' was more of a test of faith, personal strength and will. For more than a week there was no improvement in the weather. The cold, fatigue, sleeplessness and homesickness were enormous challenges. Fortunately, we were all strong and we hung in there. Eventually we decided to go down as far as Lobuje Lodge for a real rest, food and a healthy dose of oxygen. Surprisingly I think that it was there, even with all the unexpected kindness and comfort, that I felt my lowest.

Perhaps my loneliness became worse after talking to my family, and experiencing the compassion of strangers. As we walked out that morning, I lagged behind so that nobody would notice that I was crying. I cried because I felt poor, helpless and needy. Lobuje was going to be expensive, and I did not want to spoil anyone else's comforts. I confided to Kiek that I would return to Base Camp, but again his kindness saw me through and we spent three nights at the Lodge, absorbing as much oxygen and good food (potato chips, yak steak and a delicious tomato soup, all thanks to the exceptional kindness of Kiek) as we could.

At last the satellite weather station predicted good weather between 7 and 12 May. We would need to get going, and make our attempt on the summit. We headed back to Base Camp, my pace and my skin colour leading trekkers to mistake me for a sherpa.

It felt so good to be back in the place that, when we had first arrived, we thought was freezing, extreme and awful. We were to enjoy a few more rest days to focus on the final bid – and play our own, individual mind games. "Are you sure that you want to do this?" "Are you ready for the assault?" "Yes, absolutely," I said to myself, as I assured myself that there was no turning back before victory was achieved.

When a group of trekkers asked me what I thought my chances of success were I said, "One hundred percent because all the spirits of Africa will stand up and lift me to the summit."

Our first summit-bid task was to select our food rations, so that the sherpas could take them to the high camps. The team members were cautious about their choices, as they had to be something they could stomach. Most were not eating well, but I had a different story. My own strategy was to eat as much as possible to get enough energy for the challenge. It wasn't surprising then that my rations bag was the largest. While the rest of the team were selecting noodles and soups, I included rice pudding, mashed potatoes, noodles and curries, knowing that I'd eat them all.

When we started discussing our oxygen requirements, I realised just how serious things were becoming. We were split into two summit teams: the slow team and the fast team. I was to be in the slow team. I wasn't happy about this at first, but changed my mind when I heard that the fast teams would leave earlier. We intended to start at 10 pm, aim for the Balcony at 4 am, the South Summit at 7 am and Summit at 9 am.

I can still remember the heavy pounding of my heart when I saw the time: 9 am. This was it. At 9 am I would be standing on the summit. There it was – a real, concrete plan.

However, it was not yet to be. Not much can make me lose my appetite, but that's what happened when every morning I woke up, looked in the direction of the summit, and saw the cloud. A few times I simply skipped breakfast and went back to sleep in frustration.

Eventually the magical '9 am' had a date attached to it: 20 May. The weather window might open briefly, and soon would close again for the winter. We left in a hurry, climbing fast and strong to camps two, three and four. I was approaching the 'death zone' – 8 000 metres and above – for the first time.

At Camp Four, the sherpas pointed out the route – all I could see was a steep ridge of blue ice, and all I could feel was the thin, thin air. Our every movement was very slow. On my first attempt to get ice to melt, I forgot my ice axe. When I returned to my tent to fetch it, I had to rest from the exertion. Melting ice and boiling water at altitude is not easy; it seemed to take hours to melt the ice, and more hours to bring it to the boil. The cycle never seemed to stop but was a life-or-death task: at this altitude, your body is slowly dying, and liquids are all that are between you and the end.

In the late afternoon, as the sun was near setting, an ill wind started building. This was followed by a sudden drop in temperature, to an unbearable –36 to –40 °C. Our leaders confirmed our fears: no, we would not attempt the summit under these conditions. So, disappointed, there was nothing to do but sleep – if sleep is the correct word for simply lying down in your sleeping bag and staring into the dark the whole night. Again I saw the night through, hour by hour. I thought I would be frozen solid by morning, but still I still longed to take on the mountain.

The wind carried on for hours, keeping us on edge, praying that our tents would not be blown away. In the morning it was clear and chilly. Soon there was an influx of climbers and by late afternoon our peaceful camp was crowded and noisy. I had visions of a dangerous, congested route the next morning and was really worried that I would soon be defeated.

îî Victory!

"Now you have a book to write ..."

As the time to go came closer, I became preoccupied with why I was there, cold and anxious, in the death zone. I thought of my beloved family, then I prayed and dropped into my warm sleeping bag. A night up there was always going to be sleepless, even though we were using oxygen (fortified by boil-in-the-bag). I still believed that I was going to make it to the very top – on my first attempt.

At 9 pm, 20 May, we set off ... We climbed slowly, following the chain of headlamps as it wound up the mountain. There were over 150 people up there, all breathing as heavily as I was.

My worry was the congestion on the ropes. There were only two sets of ropes, and all 150 of us would be competing for them. There is no co-ordination up there, so you simply clip on to any rope.

As we progressed through the night, the wind came up again, and temperatures plummeted. It soon became apparent that we might be blown off the mountain, despite the weight of our equipment.

Some people started turning back, but no one was saying anything ...

Visibility was decreasing, and the darkness brought confusion. We were soon reduced to what we really were: scared human beings. The supremacy we had had a few minutes before was gone, and that is when our inner selves started calling for God's mercy.

The number of the people returning was growing, and included members of my team. We staggered down to the South Col in the dark, disappointed and sick!

"Injury happens when you lose focus," adventurer Ran Fiennes would tell me later. "Don't lose focus even for a few moments," he would say. "There is no room for error."

But my head was full of confusion and what did I do? I lost focus, and fell into a crevasse hidden under the powder snow. My feet were dangling about as David and some sherpas pulled me out by grabbing the shoulders of my down suit. I would still have to cross hundreds of crevasses on my way down, with this memory in my mind with every step.

We finally reached camp, a few hours before daylight. We dug into the tents and hibernated, cold, frustrated, defeated and broken.

It was 21 May and it was supposed to be the day after victory. Instead, we all saw defeat in each other's eyes.

It was then that I suspected, clearly, that this was it for me. Over. I was not a mountaineer or a climber, just a purpose-driven ordinary person who had grabbed the opportunity as it fell in my hands. Now the weather stood in my way; I realised that I was nobody fighting against the will of the Creator.

I summed it up: "Sibusiso, you were ready and well-prepared for the summit, but what prevented you was a natural event, one that you could not curb with your skills or your experience."

Yes, I was disappointed, for I was sure then that I was never going to get an opportunity like that again. The trip had cost about £37 000. I had sacrificed so much time with my family and my employers were unlikely to be so generous again …

I was sobbing bitterly as I packed my bags, getting ready for what I thought was my last ever descent of the Lhotse Face. By 7 am there was no one but me left at the camp.

The other team members were quick, and way ahead of me, but I was not bothered. My thoughts were on how I was going to face my supporters and critics on my return. I could imagine the disappointment in John's face and my family's, and I could hear the people in taxis, buses and street markets, saying, "But why did he go in the first place? Black people do not climb mountains. He thought that he could be an *umlungu* (white man)". I could not think of a defence. I had to get ready to face the music.

But, then I told myself, I did not fail on this mountain, the mountain failed me. I have been to a place I'd never dreamed of ever going, and to me that alone was an accomplishment beyond doubt.

I sighed and turned around, looking at the summit. Yes, I had set a new record for myself: 8 500 metres above sea level on foot.

The trip to Camp Two was exhausting; it took me nearly a whole day. There was not much happiness in the camp. All of us were devastated. The sherpas wanted to go home, as we had been up on the mountain for almost eight weeks. Our Camp Two cook was hoping that he'd not be at 6 200 metres for much longer. Our next move would be to pack our bags and get back to Base Camp.

But, during dinner, our leaders calculated that we had enough oxygen, and enough food, for a third attempt. On 22 May, a Korean team summitted. And the weather report said there would be good weather for the next few days.

While all this was happening, John was waiting at Base Camp – our itineraries had still not coincided, and we were corresponding only by letters. A brief radio conversation with my friend, though, was an incredible support, and I felt that John was there, climbing with me.

By the afternoon I was already at the South Col, having checked all my gear and torch batteries, spare gloves and goggles. The slow melting of ice for brew was frustrating me again, but that is how it goes.

The hour that we would start our ascent (9 pm) would be upon us again soon but, try as I might, I could not sleep. I was kept awake by the thoughts going around and around my head. How was I going to handle all the questions after the victory? I'd made quite a reverse turn in my head, from coming to terms with defeat, to imagining victory again, thinking and longing for the landmarks along the way.

Our first landmark was to be the Balcony, where we would change our oxygen tanks, then the South Summit, then the very top.

At the Balcony – in reality, no longer inside my head – everyone stopped, dropped their packs and quickly worked their apparatus. I didn't question what they were doing, but simply put down my pack and changed to a full bottle. I felt good. Some of the team were panting like lionesses that had just hunted down a buffalo, but I was fortunate to have no problem breathing.

Slowly, with determination, we each took one footstep after another. I checked my water bottle, but it had frozen. The weather was still not pleasant; it was windy and freezing, –36 to –40 °C. My ears felt as though they were going to fall off – my two balaclavas were not enough. Another persistent problem was the icing up of the oxygen mask; time and again I felt a lump on my nose, and had to use my bulky gloved hands to break the ice.

We were making good progress and I was taken back to thoughts of my family. I thought of meeting them at the airport, smiling at my wife, my son in my arms and my two princesses beaming back at me. I then came back to my senses ... and focus. Push up, man, to show that you can do this, and remember that the spirit of Africa is with you.

The order of the night became one step, breathe, one step, breathe, one step, breathe, one step ... I noticed that my climbing sherpa was lagging behind, but I pushed hard – it was the answer to the "why are you here?" question that made me feel like I was a superhuman. As the new day dawned the cloud cleared and the stars appeared.

At our second landmark – the South Summit – we were to change to a full four-litre oxygen bottle. This was the rule. It was 7.15 am and I remembered the advice of Rebecca Stephens: "If you are not at the South Summit by 11 am, turn around. Don't push yourself to the Summit if it's getting late."

My sherpa – who was carrying my spare oxygen – hadn't arrived, so I had to wait. All the other Jagged Globe tanks at South Summit were empty. Half an hour later, my sherpa arrived, and we started toward the Hillary Step.

The Step is not for the faint-hearted. I looked up and down, left and right, but I saw no easy way to conquer it. I thought that I was clipping on to rope that has been there since 1953, but later I realised that Edmund and Tenzing did not fix ropes. They probably left nothing there at all.

Eventually I reached the top of the Step, shattered and breathless. I looked around and, to my surprise, saw Camp Two right below: if I had been wearing a distinctive colour suit the *sirdar* and the cook would have known it was me up there.

I started up along the knife-edge called the Summit Ridge. Two of the climbers who had gone just ahead of me and were now going down, smiled and said, "Lion, well done, now you have a book to write!"

For a few seconds it did not make any sense. I said I would write a book only if I had conquered Everest. My fellow climber noticed my confusion: "Man, you are almost there, ten minutes more." I put on the winning smile of a proud African, shook their gloved hands and wished them a safe descent.

I looked up ahead and there she was, dressed in a snow-white dress, decorated with a few sherpa prayer flags. I saw a pillar about a metre-and-a-half tall and a group of six people standing on top. I knew then that I had succeeded!

I'd done it for Africa, done it for John and for Adam, who had paid out of his own pocket to support me, and yes, I had done it for myself, and my family. My knees weakened as I went down and prayed: "Lord, thank you for having taken me to the top of this mountain safely. I ask you Lord to take me safely back."

We viewed the world from its highest point for about a quarter of an hour. The views were as stunning as I'd imagined they would be. I felt an amazing sense of achievement at what I had done, to have climbed to the top of the world. I turned to drink in the sight from all angles, 360 degrees of nothing but unadulterated beauty. How I was blessed to be experience such a rare opportunity.

As I looked down I saw the next challenge – the path I needed to take to go back down the mountain. It looked particularly narrow and precipitous from the top. When it was time to go, I put on my rucksack, clipped myself on to the ropes and started down as Robert and David lead the way. Before long we found Fred Ziel who was still where I had passed him on the way up. David said that, as Fred was not feeling well, we should help him down. Since he was above the dangerous Hillary Step he needed more attention and the sherpas joined us to assist. We did not know exactly what exactly Fred's problem was but it was suspected that he had snow blindness and frostbite on his fingers. Slowly we descended and cleared the Hillary Step safely together.

The weather was calm now so it was easy to focus. As we reached the second step, Robert and David decided that I should go down with my climbing sherpa for help, while they stayed with Fred. I slowly carried on down the mountain. Before long I ran out of oxygen, and started to lose energy. I stopped and waited for my sherpa who was lagging behind me. When he arrived I noticed that he still had a full bottle of oxygen in his pack. I asked him to spare the bottle, to no avail, so I asked him to lead the way instead. Alas, the sherpa clearly didn't understand a word I was saying, or my hand signals, so I stood up and started walking. Soon I was hungry and thirsty, and my pace slowed to that of a snail. I had taken eleven hours to climb from the camp to the summit, yet it was becoming evident that it was going to take me almost the same time to get back down. The descent was turning into as much of an epic as the ascent. However, knowing that there was another climber in trouble, I galvanised myself. Personally I don't like going down mountains or even steep hills. Most fatal accidents happen on the descent and I was finding the climbing down as tough as the going up. It needed all my focus and alertness. I was fortunate that I had all my senses even then; I was well-oriented and in control. I tried hard not to become one of those whose concentration drifts before they disappear forever on the slopes of the mountain.

My fears were heightened by the fact that I was almost alone by the late afternoon. My sherpa was, by then, a long way behind me and I was risking getting lost or falling into a crevasse without hope of salvation. Time was ticking and I realised that, although I couldn't see them, the climbers with Fred was not making any progress whatsoever. And ours was only team still climbing down on the day.

The weather became colder, and foggy. Since the ropes were there, I stayed clipped on and followed the rope faithfully. After nine hours of gruelling descent I made it to the camp on the South Col and asked that sherpas go up to help Fred and the rest of the team. Then I joined Børge Ousland in the tent; he was already warm in his sleeping bag. He had turned back before the summit because his climbing sherpa was sick but welcomed me and congratulated me warmly on my personal victory. I was cold, hungry and very tired but I could not sleep without hot brew and food. After a long struggle I finally had boiled water and a boil-in-the-bag. Then I rigged my oxygen apparatus and drifted off to a long night's sleep.

12 Word gets out

"Every corner of this country knows your name."

> People see the pictures of Everest and think that was the hardest part.
> But for me, just getting on the expedition was the hardest part. Once
> I got on, getting to the top was just a formality ...

I had barely caught my breath back at Base Camp when I was called to the
communication tent for a satellite call ...

The voice on the other side asked, "Can you hear me, Sibusiso?"

I said "Yes, I can ... loud and clear."

"This is John Perlman, from SAFM. How are you? Do you know that
every corner of this country knows your name! We are very proud of you,
and we can't stop talking about you!"

I can so clearly recall my first reaction and it was simply this: fear! Where
would I hide from all these people ...

I knew I had wanted to show the world what could be done, but I'd been
so focused on the goal, I hadn't thought too much about the aftermath.
Now the curtains were opened, and I saw clearly what I had done.

At least John asked me an easy question next: if I were to choose a meal,
what would it be?

"Pap and vleis, of course."

A German friend on the mountain had promised me a ten-minute talk with my family, and soon he was dialling the number. The phone on the other end rang once, twice, and then I heard the voice of my darling wife. "Hello love, can you hear me? I have done it! How are you and the children?"

Nomsa had already received the news, and had been inundated by telephone calls from well-wishers she didn't even know.

"You've made us famous," she said.

What a moment! My wife was ecstatic that I was safe, and had achieved what I'd set out to do. I imagined my boy in my arms and the girls at my side – and us striding off to eat our first meal together as a family re-united (yes, food was also on my mind!).

John was back in Kathmandu by then, and was due to fly back to England a day or so later. It had been so encouraging for me that John had made the trip. Although I had hoped we could trek together for a while, I knew that each time he looked up at the mountain, he knew I was there, and that he'd put me there.

John telephoned Base Camp, and sounded as happy as if he himself had summitted. He had every reason to be so, because he had shared the dream from the day it was conceived seven years before, and he had nurtured it all the way by supporting me financially, spiritually, emotionally and physically. He'd climbed the Khumbu Icefall to Camp One, so he knew some of what I had experienced.

By 30 May we were back in Kathmandu, at the Summit Hotel. I was looking forward to a long shower and a leisurely lunch so when I heard a knock above the sound of the rushing water of the shower, I ignored it. Not long afterwards the phone rang: "There are people at reception who are looking for you, sir," said the concierge. I wondered who these people could be, and from where and why.

"I'll be down in ten minutes," I said. The visitors turned out to be journalists. I gave them my story, and then they left me to my Hawaiian burger and chips.

I arrived at Heathrow early the next morning and was met by John, who was very excited and happy. I spent nearly four days in Devon, talking and celebrating with my sponsor. Each day I received calls from journalists and from John's friends. I then left for home.

I had taken an evening flight, to arrive home the next morning – and was upgraded to business class courtesy of South African Airways. It wasn't long before a crew member appeared: "Mr Vilane, the South African government has asked that you don't speak to any media yet, but wait until your press conference in Cape Town tomorrow afternoon."

"No, I'm sorry, but I can't," I said. "I'm taking a flight straight to Swaziland to be with my family in the afternoon …"

As it happened, Minister Valli Moosa had arranged that my wife, my son and I would fly to Cape Town for the press conference and to be his guests as he delivered a speech in parliament.

When I arrived in Johannesburg, I understood what they meant about "not speaking to any media yet". I could not disembark because there were so many journalists, and I had to wait for a car and driver to speed me away.

I had suspected – hoped, of course – that my achievement would prove to be interesting to the media. However, the level of interest came as a shock. I was desperate to see my family, not only my wife and son but my girls, too. I was weary but I was also enormously happy that my country appreciated my achievement.

After about twenty minutes I made it to a lounge where I met Nomsa and Bavukile, as well as Julie and Hugh Marshall, my managers at Bongani, Shane Richardson from CCA, and a friend who was representing my sponsor. And what did we do to celebrate? We had gallons of tea, of course!

Two hours later we were on the plane to Cape Town – a first for Nomsa and Bavukile – and a round of press conferences, photographs and celebrations.

Not long after my return to work (my employers had given me extra time at home with my family), an invitation arrived to meet Baba Nelson Mandela. I was over the moon. I wondered how possible it was that I would have another dream come true. Unfortunately my precious photograph of Madiba and me together was stolen a little while afterwards.

Two weeks later I was back in parliament in Cape Town to meet President Thabo Mbeki and nine other young South African achievers. Then came the invitations to present talks at events and conferences.

Whenever I talked about my goals, and showed the photographs of the mountain, I realised that a new seed had been planted, and it was beginning to sprout. I wanted to climb again.

I remembered the words of Steve Bell at Jagged Globe: "Everest changes people, and if you get to the top you will never be the same again."

I had learnt a lesson about life and challenges. It's not your background or your race, not even your social standing, that wins in a challenge. It's your determination, perseverance and courage to face the almost impossible with the greatest of self-belief. I became increasingly certain that I could share this lesson and use it to help others.

î3 Second time around

The big thing is, what's next? What is my next challenge as a role model? I don't know what, but I must try something else – maybe in two years – to inspire the youth. Interest is huge at the school where I have been giving talks. Kids have been fascinated, asking good questions. "What did you eat?", "Who cooked for you?", "Where did you sleep?". I am thinking of returning to Everest, but the north side, and become the first to do it from both sides. If you see Sir Ranulph Fiennes, say to him, if the sponsor is there, and if he wants to climb Everest, we can team up ...

Sibusiso Vilane to John Doble, June 2003

John had always supported the dreams I'd had in the past, but he was not so certain about this one – to climb Everest from the northern, Tibetan side – especially now that he was more aware of the dangers involved in climbing at high altitude. I had accomplished that first ascent of Everest with no permanent damage to my body, but you never know what might happen a second time around.

I am pretty sure that few people think of ascending Everest more than once, just for the sake of climbing it for themselves. Guides and sherpas, of course, have a financial incentive.

I decided that I would also have a financial motive – but it would be different. I would try to generate money for charity, to assist young people.

Throughout my life I have been helped by others, by people who were not my family. For example, I might never have completed my schooling without the help of my Canadian family, the Watts. I wanted to be able to offer something to young people, too.

News was circulating that Sir Ranulph (Ran) Fiennes had just bagged another first. This time he had run seven marathons on seven continents in seven consecutive days (the Land Rover 7x7x7 Challenge) ... He'd done so after recovering from double by-pass surgery after a heart attack. To me this was a super-human achievement.

It was not long after hearing this news that I was called to the reception at Bongani Lodge, to take a telephone call. I knew it was an international call, but it was not from John.

My heart was pounding as I picked up the receiver.
"This is Sibusiso Vilane, hello."
"Sibu, this is Ran from the UK. How are you?"
"I am well, Ran and thank you for calling."
"It's all right, Sibu, and I have three things to say ..."
Firstly, he thanked me for asking him to climb Everest with me.
Secondly, he noted that he would like to climb with me if I did it for charity. He planned to choose his own organisation in the UK, and suggested I choose an organisation in South Africa.
And finally, he wanted to know how we should proceed further.
Ran had not yet spoken to his wife Ginny about the proposal, as she had recently been diagnosed with cancer. He didn't want to endanger her health or spend time away from her while she was ill.
"I promise that, should when Ginny gets better, you will hear from me."
We thanked each other and said our goodbyes. That moment I felt so rejuvenated that I sprinted up the steep hill to my quarters. My game

drive that afternoon was all fun. My spirits were high, as I thought that one day I would climb Everest again, alongside a living legend. Ran is not just a climber like me, not a mountaineer like me, but an explorer and an adventurer.

Some time later sad news was passed on to me by John. He telephoned to say that Ran's Ginny had passed away.

When interviewed about his loss, the great adventurer told the *Daily Telegraph*: "I really am terribly sorry to have lost my lovely wife and life will never be the same, but the one thing left for me now is to climb Mount Everest with an African friend of mine who had asked me to do it with him. His name is Sibusiso Vilane from South Africa."

John read this comment and he was immediately on the telephone to me. "Be warned," he said, "you may be swamped by the media!"

I waited to hear from the man himself, and the wait was not long. Ran told me that he was arranging meetings with Jagged Globe, and 2005 was the year he suggested for the climb. It would allow us at least about twelve months to prepare. Jagged Globe don't often lead trips from the north, because of the limited success rate, but Jagged Globe's Simon Lowe was a veteran of the North Ridge.

Immediately Jagged Globe arranged a series of training expeditions for Ran, similar to those I had undertaken. Ran is a great athlete and adventurer, able to push his body to extremes, but he had no experience of altitude.

Ran wrote letter after letter to obtain sponsorship. He had taken up the 7x7x7 Challenge for the British Heart Foundation, and once again they supported and sponsored some of this needs.

Anglo American agreed to cover my climbing and travelling expenses. Cape Union Mart promised gear and technical clothing, from the K-Way range. I was overjoyed. I was going to be well-dressed, and by a local company too.

In his preparation, Ran climbed Kilimanjaro and a peak in Ecuador, and did a lot of adventure racing (which includes abseiling).

I merely had the time and the budget to do a lot of psychological preparation; just thinking big and believing big! I was running about fourteen kilometres every week, supplemented by Taebo, which I really enjoyed. I didn't even get to read a book about the North Ridge.

Everything was now moving in the right direction, and I started telling people about the trip. Strangely, though, few people said it was a good decision. The reaction was mostly, "Man, that will be a difficult route to climb. Remember that very few people succeed."

Well, 'all negative' is the game I like, when I know that what I will be doing is not easy. It is then that my mind takes over and makes me believe that it is all possible.

It was in May that I officially met Alex Harris, although we'd seen each other on Everest while he was leading the Discovery Health Everest team. Alex and I shared an agent, Bronwyn Roberts, who managed our speaking-engagements. Alex confirmed his participation on the trip, as Harmony Gold agreed to sponsor him.

On each of my previous international trips I had been the one and only African – so there were no African jokes to share. I had had to be a European for a whole two months in 2003 and, although adaptability is my strength, I was really looking forward to having a fellow countryman in the team. At least I would have someone that I could look at and remember my roots.

Once again CCA supported my plan, and agreed to keep me on full pay for the three months that I was expecting to be away.

However, my mother was ill and her health was deteriorating rapidly. I visited her in Swaziland. She looked at me and said that "life is refusing". In early December she passed away. Nomsa and I managed to help my mother go to her resting place. In some way this was better than having to leave for Everest with my mother sick and dying.

Before long we were nearing February 2005. I was spending as much time as I could at Bongani Lodge to compensate for the months I would be away.

My final 'preparation', though, was a trip with my family to Hlane Royal National Park for a day visit and braai (barbecue). This was a trip that all seven children (our three and my sister's four) enjoyed very much.

As I was leaving on a week day, I had written to the school principal to ask for permission for the children to accompany me to the airport. The principal agreed and the children loved going to Nelspruit airport with Mum and Dad. I am sure it did not matter to them that I was going to take a long time to come back home. Nomsa dreaded it all, but still wished me well. She approached the situation with the bravery of a heroine.

î4 Into Tibet

A South African-dominated team

I must say that I have fallen in love with ice and snow climbing …

Sibusiso Vilane to John Doble

On the morning of 25 March, I arrived at Heathrow once again. I was happy that I was to spend the day with John. It's always special for us to meet, and this time was no exception.

The check-in personnel at the airport in Johannesburg had been horrified by the amount of baggage I was carrying and I had to pay a substantial sum for being 26 kilograms overweight. Whatever made me think that that same baggage was going to fit into John's Morgan, I don't know. Fortunately John had brought ropes to tie the bags onto the boot of the car, while we squeezed the rest of them in behind us.

The day was clear, so we had the roof down and wore woollen balaclavas to keep out the cold air. We spent the four-hour trip to Devon talking about our day-to-day lives, and catching up. I was to be there for just the one day, as we would be departing for Everest on the evening of 26 March. This time, though, John would also be climbing Everest – not to the top, but as high as he could get.

David Hamilton was to lead this expedition; this was a second meeting for us as we were together in 2003.

Three days after I had arrived in London I was once again at the Summit Hotel in Kathmandu. And once again I began my diet of tea (lots of liquid) and food that was rather different to my usual fare. After a breakfast of omelette and fruit salad, I was fortified for my first task in Nepal: to be interviewed by Elizabeth Hawley.

Elizabeth, an American national, has been described as one of the most important figures in Himalayan climbing – even though she has never actually been to Everest Base Camp. In 1960 she moved to Kathmandu as a reporter for *Time* and still lives in the city, having written about almost every expedition to the Nepalese Himalayas since.

She was interested in my reasons for climbing Everest a second time, to which I gave my now usual answer: "I'm attempting to try the North Ridge to raise funds for charity."

This second trip to Kathmandu was different to my first in many ways, not least because this time I had a better idea of what to expect, and because I did not have to buy boots or much other equipment – just memory sticks for my digital cameral and film for my 'normal' camera.

By now another South African had joined us, which meant that 'we' dominated the nationalities. Ran also regarded himself as a South African – having spent his formative years in South Africa – so there were four of us. Mark Campbell, our new compatriot, was a friend of Alex's, and had attempted the North Ridge route in 1996. I liked him immediately, as he looked determined but cheerful.

The following day we commenced the ten-day journey to Base Camp on the Tibetan side. In 2003, we had flown to Lukla, then walked to Base Camp. This time we would take a bus to the border between Tibet and Nepal, then travel by 4x4 to Base Camp.

We were, of course, accompanied by an extraordinary load of bags, and our team of fifteen sherpas (cooks, carrying sherpas and climbing sherpas).

Our *sirdar* was a man named Nima Gombu. He had an excellent reputation, having summitted Everest ten times, as well as a number of other 8 000 metre peaks. In fact his entire family has a reputation on Everest – our team had four of his brothers, with 26 Everest summits between them.

We hit the road speeding! Our driver manoeuvred through forests and windy roads, up and down hills, for hours. Some sections were scary indeed, as the road became more and more narrow, but not any less busy. I closed my eyes every time another bus passed ours on the road, and tried to block out the hooting as drivers approached the numerous sharp corners. Every ten kilometres or so, we were confronted by yet another safety hazard, a security checkpoint manned by armed officers.

After three hours of travel I was desperate to pee. This is a typical response to being at high altitude and drinking lots of liquid, but on a bus you don't usually keep a pee bottle with you. I asked the driver for a break, but we had a wait for one of the rare safe places to stop. I jumped from the bus and, to my surprise, the whole busload of people followed me for the same purpose.

An hour or so later we stopped for lunch at a tea house. While we savoured our freshly-cooked meal of lentils, rice and chicken, we watched the buses pass by. Clearly no one issues fines for overloading; even the top of the buses were crammed with passengers.

Our journey continued for another five or six hours, without much conversation. We were still mostly strangers to one another. I was seated next to sherpas whom I had met before, so we would chat between naps stolen on the less bumpy sections of gravel road.

Rivers flowed strongly from the mountain slopes, while houses and rice or barley fields were positioned at seemingly impossibly steep angles. The road kept winding up the mountain, past roadworks and new tea houses and lodges which were still being constructed. Suddenly the number of houses increased, evidence that we were nearing the village of Kodari, and the end of our first day of travel.

The next day we proceeded, without complication, through the Nepalese border, and walked across the famous bridge that marks the border to Chinese-controlled Tibet. There was a very long queue and, as travellers often do, we started recording the experience on camera. In no time we heard officials shout: "No camera, no photo!"

Mean-looking men in green uniforms maintained a watchful eye on us for the rest of our time in the queue. We all managed to get our passports stamped, before being pushed forward to the next checkpoint. There, nothing happened ... We waited and waited. We yawned, we thirsted and we starved, without respite or mercy. Three hours later our queue had still gone nowhere.

Eventually we were directed into an office which was like a crime investigation room. Here our bags were scanned, our passports and visas checked, and re-checked and our patience tried with questions and more questions. We South Africans were pushed to one side to wait, and our documents were further scrutinised, but we were offered no explanation. All that we cherished was the go-ahead signal. Eventually, exhausted and with nerves frayed, we were left to proceed.

Our Chinese drivers were waiting in five Land Cruisers, bound for a place called Nyalam. All the vehicles pulled off in convoy, the road as windy as ever and the day cold and patchy with snow. Along the way we passed ruined monasteries which had been destroyed by the Chinese.

In the late afternoon I noticed that we were gaining altitude and the vegetation was getting more and more sparce. We were getting closer to the 'no life' zone. The roads and mountains were full of snow.

Eventually we pulled into the five-star hotel that was to be our home for two nights. It was quite an establishment – unusually big and crowded for Himalayan accommodation.

We were warned to be aware of dogs – they are all over the place, and they bite as they please. It was suggested that we always a stone in our hand as a discouragement. I quickly adopted that idea, for I was once bitten as a teenager.

I shared a room with Mark and Alex, and meals were served across the street. These were Chinese-style, with chopsticks. I did not frustrate myself trying to use the sticks to eat. A spoon worked much better. Although the food was edible, I struggled at morning meals, as the bread and omelettes or fried egg did not go down well with me.

The one thing that puts me off on these expeditions is the ablutions. No matter what the 'star' rating of the accommodation, the toilets are all the same: unpleasant, unwelcoming, and unbearable. Is it a surprise, then, that I opted for cups of tea and no food at all?

15 Getting acclimatised, again

Where attitude and adaptability count most

At Nyalaus we began our programme of day hikes, climbing high, then sleeping low. Each day our only discipline was to walk slowly, do everything slowly and with caution. The order of the day became: wake up, eat, walk, read, sleep, eat, walk, read …

We did not talk much to each other, apart from "How are you?" and "Let's go for lunch" or "Do you want some Pringles?" We were still getting to know each other and reluctant to dig deep in conversation. Mark and I would loudly sing Mzekezeke's song 'Akekho Ugogo' together; we tried to teach Alex, but the man's tongue is so hard!

On one of our walking days, as I entered a tea house for lunch, someone called out my name. I couldn't see anyone I recognised, but then I saw someone smiling at me from a corner. "Sibusiso, I am Richard," he said. "I wanted to meet you." He was another South African, climbing Everest with another team. Such meetings are always a pleasure for me.

After the two days at Nyalaus we continued by vehicle to Tingri, closer to Base Camp. At about midday we came to a pass where we had the best views so far of Cho Oyu, Everest and Shishapangma. The white plume was visible on Everest, and brought back memories of 2003.

Tingri was to be our home for four days. The landscape reminded me of the Drakensberg and the Barberton mountains and, of course, I thought of my family at home.

Six of us shared a room and, as I really like my privacy, those four days seemed like a month! However, our room was sheltered and better than a tent, and the food was excellent: rice with vegetables or chicken, and chapatis.

At sunset I noticed diesel trucks pulling in to park near our hotel. I didn't think about them again, until dawn ... As it was, I didn't sleep well (on account of our shared room), but when the trucks began to warm their engines in readiness for the day, it became unbearable. The fumes were sickening. I thought I was going to suffocate in my sleeping bag. Everyone complained about the situation over breakfast, so I realised that I was not the only one suffering.

The morning was lovely, though, so after breakfast we went for our day hike. Unfortunately most of us were starting to feel headachy.

I managed to chat briefly to my wife on the phone. Calls are charged in dollars, which is why the chat was very short! My family was missing me, and course I was missing them.

Some climbing teams left Tingri and freed up a few rooms. This was good news, of course, so I moved into a room with Alex. Although I still didn't have the best of sleeps, I understood that lack of sleep is my particular problem on high-altitude climbs. I didn't panic but it did worry me that I had begun coughing. Most of us were developing a high-altitude cough, known as the 'Khumbu Cough' on the south side of Everest. I told myself that it would stop on its own, without medication.

At dawn the next day, the trucks were at it again. This time, however, the sound of the engines was accompanied by loud shouting. The accent sounded familiar. "Hey man, go or stop it. Why do you start if you are not going?" It was Mark, giving the drivers a piece of his mind. Perhaps it was a good thing that we couldn't understand the drivers' responses.

On our return to camp that day, after our walk, we passed three good-looking, well-dressed figures. Neal commented that one of them looked like Ed Viesturs. I turned my head to look at them again, thinking that it would be a good opportunity to speak to the famous American climber. Too late, they were gone.

At camp other climbers confirmed that the group did indeed include Viesturs, the only American to have climbed all fourteen mountains in the world higher than 8 000 metres without supplemental oxygen. At this point he was on his way to climb his fourteenth peak – Annapurna.

Alex, in the meantime, was on his way to climb the highest point in his immediate neighbourhood. I had watched him become increasingly desperate to telephone home, but in Tingri, satellite reception was not good. Fortunately, Alex's problem-solving skills don't suffer at altitude. It wasn't long before he was on the roof of a nearby house, talking to his lady as if he had not spoken to her for a year.

On 5 April, we were at last ready to leave for Base Camp. Our Land Cruisers were still in good shape and ready to 'snow and roll'.

A few hundred metres from one of Tibet's few active monasteries (Rongbuck), we saw what must be the best-ever distant view of Everest. There she was, standing tall, as beautiful as a queen indeed. For a full five minutes none of us said a word. To me, Everest was looking at me with her arms wide open saying, "You are welcome again, Sibusiso, after two years".

I turned and looked at Alex. "What are you thinking?"

"She looks big, but this time I will summit her," he said.

At Base Camp it was every man to a tent and each of us could enjoy some privacy for a change. And at least here I was going to eat what the sherpas cooked – dahl, and porridge.

Base Camp on the south side is rough and rugged; on the north side, the camp is open, barren, flat. The way we moved was the same: laboured and slow. The wind began to howl almost as soon as we arrived.

At least we'd made it to Base Camp and, I thought, I'd better get used to the surroundings.

Again, our sherpas had done a tremendous job putting up the camp, complete with a cook's tent, mess tent and communications tent. We even had latrines. The sherpas uplifted my spirit when I saw how they performed in such barren conditions. How could I not find the commitment to climb the mountain?

Over dinner that first night, David briefed us about logistics and our climbing programme. Ran and I were the only team members with limited technical climbing experience, yet we were the two team members with the highest media profiles. However, it seems that past experience doesn't count too much on Everest: it's your attitude and your ability to adapt to the challenge that makes the difference.

16 Adapting ...

... to the challenge ahead

Life at Base Camp was rather different to my experience two years before – and not only because of the landscape. This time, I felt more at ease with the people on our team, and felt I had something to contribute. Nobody could accuse me now of not being a team-player – although I would always be someone who enjoyed his own company and space.

Our plan was to complete some hikes around Base Camp – a few hundred metres higher – then move on to Advance Base Camp once everyone felt comfortable. The next goal was to get to Camp One at 7 000 metres. This would signal the end of our acclimatisation schedule and only then could we start to aim for the summit.

By now we were beginning to get to know each other well, and long, engaging conversations were the order of the day. I hadn't travelled like the other members of the team and didn't have entertaining stories to tell about journeys and adventures across the globe. However, I found my niche on the subject of wildlife, game viewing and birding, and I found a ready audience for my stories of encounters with buffaloes and lions in Africa. I felt very much part of the party there.

I had spoken to Nomsa a number of times since arriving and was, of course, happy to know that all was well at home.

Every day the weather was similar. The morning sky would be clear and blue, the air slightly warm. As the day progressed, the weather would slowly deteriorate and clouds would build up in the sky. In the evening the wind would pick up, and after sunset we could not escape the need for down jackets and fleece trousers.

This pattern made it possible to plan the day's activities: a walk in the morning, and rest and reading in the afternoon. Most of us were coughing, but I still wasn't taking my cough seriously.

Meanwhile, our sherpas had started to transport gear and equipment to Intermediate Camp and Advance Base Camp. These camps were situated at the altitudes of 6 000 metres and 6 500 metres respectively. As Advance Base Camp was about twenty kilometres from Base Camp, we would make our way up via Intermediate Camp, over two days.

A week after our arrival, we had participated in the traditional Puja ceremony, as I had on the south side, and the sherpas were now happy to work above Base Camp. We were approaching the second week of April, and our team was doing well.

More teams had begun arriving at camp, and we met a number of interesting people, including two Indian teams – an all-woman army team and an airforce team – as well as a Norwegian team and a Russian expedition. The biggest commercially-organised expedition was run by New Zealander Russell Bryce, with about 20 clients, four guides and 40 sherpas. Among his group was a Canadian I had met two years before, Peggy Foster. Then there were various small groups and individual climbers, without sherpas or oxygen.

On 12 April we agreed to move toward Advance Base Camp, via an interim Camp One and Intermediate Camp. So began the weighing of the yak loads (so that the loads weren't too heavy), and packing and sending our gear and clothing up to Advance Base Camp. Thankfully, our cook would be with us at each of the camps.

Our route along the East Rongbuk Glacier has been named Mallory's 'Magic Highway'. The route was well worn, and easy to follow, although not as worn as the south side. We crossed a frozen stream several times and walked on solid ice at various points. Most eye-catching of all was the glacier itself, and three-storey-high towers of blue ice: seracs or ice pinnacles. By the late afternoon, though, I was so tired and worn out that I could hardly walk. I have never been so tired in my life.

The next morning we had to do it all over again, to get to Advance Base Camp. The last 200 metres before camp were the most demanding; I had never struggled to finish a short distance like that before. I almost crawled on all fours to get to camp. This technique proved to be a good idea, as the terrain of moraine and rubble is so treacherous that, while walking upright, one could break an ankle at any moment.

Advance Base Camp was large and well-organised. Our mess tent – always a highlight for me – was comfortable, with tables and camping stools. Rice and fresh vegetables were on the dinner menu and my appetite was still sharp. Unfortunately, the porridge, something I had been looking forward to, was full of nuts and various other things I was not used to. Everyone else seemed to like this muesli-porridge though, so I was back to having nothing for breakfast.

Back at Base Camp I had another chance to talk to my wife and some of my friends. I also received some inspiring news about the charities, and the plan for a 'telethon' campaign. I managed to telephone John to warn him about the challenges as he prepared to come to Everest sometime in May.

I am a slow reader, which might be a good thing on a journey such as this. I was still reading *Facing Up: A Remarkable Journey to the Summit of Everest* by Bear Grylls. At the age of 23, he was the youngest Briton to summit Everest. I was finding it enjoyable but it took a while as I was reading it together with my scriptures.

Two years before I had finished the New Testament that Penny Watt had sent me from Canada, but I had left it behind this time and was not at all happy. I had mentioned this to Alex, who decided to give me a present of one of his two Bibles. I treasured the gift, read it every day, and vowed that I would take it to the top. In between reading I would sleep, or respond to summonses from the mess tent which announced the meals of the day.

Each team member had his own preferred way of passing the time. Alex, Ran, Mark and Ian Parnell enjoyed playing a card game called 'hearts'. (As time passed, I was taught to play bridge.) Like me, some were 'tent people' who kept their eyes glued to each chapter of the book they wanted to finish.

Tore Rasmussen's books were in Norwegian, so he could not exchange them with anyone. No one seemed interested in exchanging books with me either. My 'bookshelf' included *A Long Walk to Freedom* by Nelson Mandela, a book that most souls surely have read once or twice; *Martin Luther King, Jr., on Leadership: Inspiration and Wisdom for Challenging Times* by Donald Phillips, *The Power of a Praying Wife* by Stormie Omartian; and, of course, Alex's Bible. Alex was going through books quickly, and his pile of already-read books was growing every day. The corner of our mess tent was beginning to look like a bookstall.

Digital reading matter, on the other hand, proved to be a let-down. Our Base Camp had no access to the internet, as the computers had not coped well with the altitude. As a letter-writer and book-reader, I was not too bothered by this, but my team mates were disappointed. And, of course, we needed the internet for weather updates, and to send daily dispatches to the Jagged Globe website. Things were almost as primitive as John's Devon farm! Neither of us really knew what the buttons on a computer keyboard were for. My wife would say, *"Yini yona le inthanethi?"* (What is this internet?) if anyone asked whether she checked the internet for news on our progress on Everest.

Around camp there were a number of stone cairns that had been created in memory of the climbers who lost their lives on the mountain. These were humbling sights, with names of the real pioneers on them: Joe Tasker, Peter Boardman, George Mallory ...

On a rest day I stood near one of these memorials and looked in the direction of Everest. There she was, looking as innocent as could be. Then I looked around camp and saw the hundreds of people who hoped to stand at her summit and come back alive. I feared that not all of us were going to return to our loved ones but, as to which of us was going to join these heroes, Everest would neither tell nor signal. She keeps it a secret until she eats you, and then you know that you are the victim.

I felt sure, however, that she had whispered this message to me: "You will return to Africa to tell your story for the Africans who need tales like yours to boost their confidence."

After a week of resting at Base Camp, our second acclimatisation climb to Advance Base Camp was due. I was happy about this progress, but my cough was becoming frustrating. At times I could not finish a sentence but I managed to telephone Nomsa, and let her know that I was safe. I spoke to Bronwyn, too, and she told me that she had found a publisher for my story.

17 Waiting ...

... for the 'window'

The second week of May was the week in which John and his team would trek to Base Camp, then upward to the North Col. I had been looking forward to meeting up with John, and hoped that he would find us still at Base Camp.

I was in my tent when I heard two engines roar, signalling the arrival of the Land Cruisers, and there was John. He was so fit and well that he accompanied us on a scheduled two-hour walk towards Everest, along the main route to Camp One.

John's arrival provided me with additional motivation. He was there because I was there. He is indeed the best of mentors. He lifted up my spirits in so many ways. His presence was a blessing. He is part of me; he is my family, a brother and a friend indeed.

Our discussions were now centred around the next move, our summit attempt. We would move up to Advance Base Camp (6 500 metres) and wait for the window of opportunity. The actual summit was still about four camps above Advance Base Camp, and to cover this 2 348 metres of altitude would require about five days of aggressive climbing. Of course, the window opens and closes as it pleases, so you have to be in the right place and ready to capitalise on it. The window can last a day or a week, and technology doesn't really help with the timing. Although we had not yet received good weather reports, we decided to start moving up.

John had visited a Tibetan market at the entrance to Base Camp, and had purchased a carpet which provided exceptional warmth in his tent. He announced that he was going to take it up to the Advance Base Camp to sleep on, and then take it back to England.

When I arrived at the next camp at 6 000 metres, John and his team were already settled in. As much as they were excited about the experience, John said that day had not been their best. He was indeed exhausted and was, at that moment, finding his high altitude carpet very comforting.

My health was still good, except for the coughing. I did not stop for lunch but was constantly drinking fluids.

Getting to Advance Base Camp was torture and, when I arrived, there was no news on summit dates. The weather was terrible; the winds were strong, blowing over the ridge and the summit itself.

Expedition leaders moved from one team to the next, asking for reports. For days we simply received forecasts of high winds every day.

I spent my time resting, then walking above Advance Base Camp. This camp was as busy as a trading area, a small town abuzz with activity. No one really pays attention to anyone else. David maintained that this time we would try for one attempt, and he urged us to maintain our focus and patience.

A few days later, John's party passed our tents. I assured them that I would follow and hoped to catch up with them at the 'crampon area' above Advance Base Camp. Half an hour later I took my pack and followed them. The day was overcast, misty and wet. As I caught up with the team I identified one of the figures ahead of me as John. He was worryingly slow: step and stop, step and stop … until I caught up with him.

John was exhausted but determined. I did not want to climb to the Col without him on this day, so I opted to stay with him and climbed at his pace. I so wanted to see my brother and friend on the famous North Col. We clipped our jumars and cowstails onto the ropes, put on our packs and slowly ascended.

John was great; he has amazing willpower. He dealt with some of the difficult sections with confidence.

By late afternoon we had reached 6 900 metres, only 100 metres short of Camp One. However, the weather had become unbearable, so we turned back to Advance Base Camp. We maintained our focus and arrived at the tents safely where, of course, we enjoyed plenty of tea. John bid me goodbye and descended to his campsite because his group was going to return to the Base Camp the following morning.

I was sad to see him go.

The weather not only defeated John, but it looked as though it was going to defeat us too. Our plans for advancement seemed to come to a halt, and most of the teams decided to leave the camp. Campsites opened up as yaks arrived to haul equipment and belongings out. We were still content, but the waiting was tough. We had been on the mountain for almost 60 days and had hoped to be home by now.

Fortunately, our team spirit simply grew stronger. We joked that if we had to we'd stay for the whole of June. I hoped that I could maintain such motivation for other life challenges.

May 30 was to be the start of our final assault, and we were hoping to summit on 3 June. I envisaged myself coming down on 4 June, my mind brimming with a sense of achievement and excitement.

I had been allocated a young sherpa who had summitted Everest twice. He was quiet, but spoke English well. I had no doubt that we were going to make it. Alex and I had only two camps to go, then victory. I was sleeping on oxygen, and it was a good feeling to be counting down to summit day.

Our itinerary had set Camp Two at 7 500 metres, but we agreed that Team A (my team) would pass the 7 500 metre camp and stay over at 7 900 metres – an eight or nine hour climb. On arrival, we devoured our boil-in-the-bag rations and zipped ourselves into our sleeping bags. However, no sleep came as the wind grew stronger. I watched as the tent fabric flapped against the gusts. If the wind did not drop, we would be going back in the morning. Alex and I were sharing a tent, but we could not talk to each other as the sound of the wind was deafening.

When morning broke, I thought David was going to tell us to descend to Camp One, but instead he suggested that we spend one more night here. Our high-altitude sherpas had failed to climb even 100 metres away from camp. I could see the frustration and uncertainty in their eyes as they were blown off their feet while trying to reach our Camp Three, at 8 300 metres. While we waited, I received a call from a Cape-based radio station on David's satellite phone; they wanted to know of my progress, but the conditions were so bad that I could not hear a thing.

18 My return to the extreme

Not much air to breathe, let alone sing!

Our main concern was whether or not we had enough oxygen. Although we didn't have much food, we also didn't have huge appetites. Oxygen, however, was a crucial ingredient in our recipe for success and survival. We had enough to see us through one more night, but probably not another. Eventually David determined that we would move on up to the next camp the following day, no matter what.

Yes! Yes! I punched the air as I heard the announcement; it was all that I wanted to hear from our leader.

By nightfall we had eaten and were cocooned in our sleeping bags. We endured another night of terror but, as it is said, "The day shall dawn". We were also reducing our oxygen intake as we slept ... one litre per minute while sleeping, but two litres per minute while climbing.

The wind was still blowing strongly as we left camp. It threatened to blow us off the mountain and, at one stage, I noticed myself getting blown off the route. Fearing for my life, I gripped the rope, and slowly gained some height and distance. We were facing at least four or five hours of climbing – and only 400 metres of vertical altitude gained ...

Since the day has been so difficult to deal with, our sherpas had not been able to climb any faster than we had. When I got to the camp at 8 300 metres, they were still battling to put up the tents. I was to share with Alex again. The wind was blowing, and wind-shredded tents were everywhere. I looked towards Everest and the route appeared clearly along a steeply-sloping rocky ridge. The mountain was clear in all directions. We were above the clouds, above many mountains and, indeed, I was above my 'self-being'. I was still well, and tried to settle in my tent. Our summit-start time, 11 pm, was not far away.

I had all my belongings at my feet and used my pack as a pillow, but there was not enough space for me to lie down. I rested in a semi-sitting position and confronted the next problem: to melt, and boil, enough water for the summit push.

The tent's outer door had been torn into pieces, so we could not light the gas stoves in the entrance; the cold would have been unbearable. We were compelled to cook inside, and this took up valuable resting space. Alex was desperate to sleep, so I boiled just two litres of water and cleared away the stove – I was more used to drinking four litres a day, but two would have to do. Alex's restless sleeping habits had once before knocked over a stove, and I was not going to risk this again!

I ate my boil-in-the-bag dinner, took a few photographs of the sunset, and checked my oxygen apparatus. Then I put my gloves and socks in the sleeping bag, and tried to rest.

When the summit summons arrived, I hadn't really slept, and had been worrying about my water. But I put on my harness, picked up my camera, checked my spare torch batteries, and went out into the night.

David, Tore, Alex and myself were the only summit team up on the north side that day. Team B would be along sooner or later. It was easy to follow the route, but it demanded a hundred percent performance and focus.

The route shot up a ridge, toward the north-east, then traversed south toward the first step. As we neared the top of the ridge, the weather changed to overcast, although visibility was still excellent. And what a view: it was the first time I had ever seen lightning on such big mountains. I have seen beautiful lightning in Africa, stretching for miles across the horizon, but this Himalayan electricity was very special.

It was then that I noticed that my sherpa was climbing very slowly. I stopped to find out if he was all right. No, he was not, he said, as his breathing apparatus was not working very well. He had a very old mask and the regulator was leaking. We tried to tape it, but it still did not work. Then he remembered that he had a spare regulator in his backpack. It took him ages to untape the regulator from the leaking mask. He was freezing in the cold and, to make things worse, he cut his finger with my penknife. I could no longer see the headlamps of the other members. At last we fixed his oxygen set and continued climbing, after a good 40-minute delay. And in the 'thin air zone', you can't make up time once you've lost it.

We plodded on, over the first step, and eventually I saw headlamps way ahead of us. They remained in the same spot for quite some time. As we got closer we saw that the bottleneck was at the notorious second step. I arrived just as Alex disappeared above it and was gone.

We then faced the step ourselves. It is a technically demanding obstacle. my sherpa led the way, and I followed in his steps and grips. It was a test of our skills, common sense and ability. We knew about the aluminium ladder up ahead, at the second step, and yes, it was indeed a wonderful idea by the Chinese and the South Africans to put up that ladder. But getting to the ladder is the tricky bit, and the traverse once one gets to the top of the ladder is something else. In hindsight I can say that it was a fun experience, but at the time it took a long time to clear the second step. And, if you make a mistake there, it'll probably be the last one you'll ever make!

Despite – or perhaps because of – its dangers and challenges, experiencing the wildness of Everest was the highlight of my summit bid. At night, all I could see was the mountain. No town or city lights. I love that about mountain climbing in places like the Himalayas.

When daylight broke, we were dealing with the last of the steps – the third. This was not difficult. Visibility was clear in every direction, and I saw David, Tore, Alex and sherpas Mingma and Passang just below the summit pyramid, climbing the steep snow and ice ridge. They were climbing strongly. We followed.

Suddenly I was confronted by the body of a dead climber. The sight really brought home to me the danger of what we were doing. I was five metres away when I saw him, clipped to the same rope as myself, face up, with his head below his feet. His pack was about a metre away. He appeared well preserved, having been frozen in time. I felt weak in my knees as I considered his fate. Oh my God, I thought, what wrong did he do and what right am I going to do? I had no answer but to trust and believe in God, that I was there in His mercy, that my being there was a calling from the Lord and that He would guide me safely. I said a quiet prayer for the climber, unclipped from the rope so I could pass his body, then clipped in again on the other side and carried on.

I checked my watch and it was going on 6 am. The sun was rising. I took some pictures, and turned on my radio so I could hear David calling Base Camp when they got to the top. It was only half an hour later that we heard him make the call.

I was particularly happy for Alex. He had now achieved his dream of joining the exclusive Seven Summits club. Well done to him – Everest at last! Then I switched off the radio and kept going higher and faster, for I thought David might turn us back if we did not get there soon. By then I could see them on the summit, as they celebrated by taking pictures of one another.

As we got closer, we perfected our slow-motion climb, a very slow plod, until the summit appeared and I sped up to join the others and to pose for a picture.

This time, I looked around me carefully, and remembered what I had seen two years ago. I had not noticed, then, that the routes to the top never meet. The only thing they have in common is the thin air.

While at the top I did something I had wanted to do for a long time: to sing 'Nkosi Sikelel' iAfrika' from the top of the world while holding my symbol of hope and prosperity, a copy of *The Long Walk to Freedom* (the abridged version, of course). It is almost impossible to sing when there is no air to breathe. I had to take off my oxygen mask, and soon I was gasping. Eventually I recovered and spent half an hour on the surprisingly small summit (it's big enough for only two people) without reaching for my oxygen.

Again Everest had given me one of the best of all experiences. The visibility was perfect and it was actually fairly warm. What a blessing! I gave thanks to the Lord for this once in a lifetime opportunity.

Then David ordered us to start down.

19 The even longer walk down

Hope has no fail.

It was just after 7 am. It had been a good time to summit and we each descended at our own pace. My sherpa and I were last, but the rest of the team was still within sight.

Then I started getting very, very thirsty, in a way that I'd never experienced before. By 10 am, the excitement of my successful summit had been put aside by my thirst.

I pushed my hand into my pack, and fiddled about until I found my water bottle. I took it out and tried to squeeze the last drops from it. There were none, not a single drop. The half-filled bottle had frozen and I had had nothing to drink since 11 pm. I was tired, hungry and, eventually, very irritable. My cough was also bad.

At around midday I reached the highest camp – in time to see Alex and his yellow daypack vanish out of sight. I collapsed in our tent, my feet out the door, my crampons still on.

I lay there without water, and nothing much to eat, too exhausted to do anything. I hoped that the sherpas would check on me. After half an hour a sherpa shouted: "Sibu, we are going down."

"I need water," I replied.

"OK," he said. "Five minutes."

Five minutes passed, and no water.

David and Tore left camp, passing my tent. "We're going down now. You have to pack up," they said. "And you'll have to carry your own things as the sherpas are carrying the oxygen."

Then they disappeared, too, to Camp One.

"Sibu, we go," the sherpas shouted. "But I need water," I gasped.

A sherpa came into the tent, took some of Alex's things, and vanished. I felt as if I had been left for dead.

At about 2 pm, I shook myself awake, packed my things and dragged myself out of the tent. I had no energy. None. My knees were shaking. I could not lift my bag. For a few minutes I thought of my family, then I took out the hand radio and called Base Camp. I asked for Gianni, the camp manager. "Please call my wife, John, and Bronwyn, and tell them the lion has done it again. Please tell my wife that I am now down to safety."

Little did I know what hell lay before me.

I dragged my bag out of the tent and put it beside me. My legs were so wobbly and weak that I fell on my bum. I could not believe how physically weak I was. I sat outside the tent, looking down the mountain, and I saw two climbers arriving at Camp Three.

I just stared at them, and I am sure the expression in my eyes was full of terror. I tried to greet them, but they signalled "hello" instead of saying it.

"Do you have water?"

"What?" the first man said.

I repeated: "Do you guys have water to spare?"

They were not English-speaking, but intent on trying to understand. They came closer, and I repeated my plea. They each gave me half a cup.

It turned out that the two were the 'speedy Italians', one of whom was trying to break the record for the fastest ascent of all seven summits. They had saved a life with their generosity. Then they took their bags, said their goodbyes, and I bowed to thank them.

Soon afterwards, Ran Fiennes and his sherpa, Nima Dorje, pulled into camp. I waited for Nima to put down his bags, then I called him. My eyes filled with tears. I asked him to please help me put on my crampons. I said that his brothers had left me for dead without water, without food and without support.

He was perplexed to see me like this. He had known me to be polite and ever smiling, but how things had changed. I was more than desperate. He quickly dressed me up and I asked him to help me lift my pack. He very kindly did so, then led me to the ropes. What an honourable man.

I staggered slowly along, and about 200 metres from the camp I started encountering the rest of Team B. They greeted me with excitement, and congratulated me on my successful summit. I was close to tears as I realised quite how serious my situation was. By the time I met the last member of the group, Ian Parnell, I was weeping. He not only offered me a drink of water, but sacrificed his full water bottle to me. Another gentleman. I thanked him and down the route of hell I went.

Slowly the mountain became desert-still. And then the wind started howling. Like a tension spring that suddenly loses power, my energy dropped to zero. The pack felt ten times heavier. I could not carry it.

There was nobody near me by then.

I remembered the radio. I sat down to call Advance Base Camp. When Stephanie responded, I asked for a sherpa to help me. "I have a problem," I explained, but she did not hear me. I suddenly had a fit of coughing. She signalled that she had not received my message. I tried to relay it again, but in vain. So I dropped the radio back into the pack; I was wasting my last ounce of energy and time over nothing.

I started down again, one step at a time, and then it did not feel possible anymore – I had run out of oxygen. Running out of oxygen at high altitude is a death sentence. The music of the devil was sounding very clear.

I thought, "Well, well, well. This is it, Sibusiso." Realising that I could not accept my fate, I adopted the Joe Simpson style of descent: I slid down on my bum, having clipped my pack to my harness. It was not the best method, but I gained some distance as the sun started to disappear behind the mountain.

Time was running out; this game is only played during daylight. If the sunset and I were on the mountain together, then I was a dead man.

At about 4 pm my cough got much, much worse. I could not breathe, and started to feel overwhelmingly sleepy. I sat for a few seconds to catch my breath, and suddenly started falling asleep. It occurred to me that this is why climbers are often found dead in a simple sitting position ... I decided I would not die sitting. So I shook myself and carried on with the bum slide. I told myself that since I had taken myself up there, then the task was mine to save my life. Then I burst out weeping again. I'd made one stupid mistake – by not putting enough effort into making drinking water – and I might be paying with my life.

The wind picked up and it started to blow into my face, making it diffi-cult to see, but I was assured that for as long as I carried on paddling along on my bottom, I would not die.

Both camps were beyond sight now and I was in the middle of nowhere, in the dark shadow of the mountain. Soon I would be in darkness.

So it was that 3 June 2005 became equally the most uplifting and the most challenging day of my life.

Suddenly I saw a person, a sherpa, coming towards me from the high camp. I felt a glimmer of hope: perhaps I could ask this man to carry my pack down to Camp Two (7 900 metres). It is said that hope has no fail.

"Hello, my friend," I said.

He mumbled something back.

"Can you help me carry this bag to the next camp for $50?"

"No," he replied. "$150."

"OK, that's fine, but I don't have the money here. It is at Advance Base Camp and I am with Jagged Globe, so I will give you $150 there."

He looked at me in the face and calmly said, "No. Cash now." And then he strode past me and vanished over the ridge. I was left aghast.

Now it's me and the mountain, I thought – and this thought brought more tears. And when the snow became moraine scree, my bum felt the sting. How else could I manage. I contemplated abandoning my pack but then I remembered that it contained my sleeping bag, which might come in handy later, and spare goggles. Most importantly it held my camera with the precious photos from earlier in the day.

But angels are everywhere.

The sun had set. I was gingerly bumping down some more scree, when I thought I heard a voice. Could it be someone shouting my name?

"Sibusiso!"

Away the sound went with an echo.

I stopped panting and listened. I could not figure out the direction from which the sound was coming. Perhaps it was the ghost of Mallory or Irvine? There had been reports of ghosts around the camps. Or perhaps I was simply imagining things.

I paused again, and then I turned and looked behind me. A dark figure was moving towards me. I sat there waiting for him, but I was crying. Weeping more bitterly than ever before.

The sherpa caught up with me, and sat beside me, panting like an exhausted lion. He fumbled in his pack and took out a radio. There was a response from the high camp. He spoke Nepali, but I understood that I was about an hour from Camp Two.

This angel was none other than the young Mingma. He was to be Mark Campbell's climbing sherpa that very same night, but he had come to look for me. He had sacrificed his chance of summitting Everest, and Mark would attempt to summit without a sherpa. This act was a supremely humane and generous one. Without Mingma and Mark, I am certain that this book would have been published posthumously.

Afterword

Mark did make it to the top, sharing one of Ran's two sherpas.

Ran turned back at about 8 400 metres. He had set off an hour earlier than the rest for the summit attempt but, about 400 metres above the high camp, he felt an uncomfortable pain in his chest. He recognised it as a possible heart attack. "I had to choose between life and death. So I chose life, and that is why I am here," he said later.

Tore, at 56 years of age, became the oldest Scandinavian person to summit Everest.

Our certificates, and our names on them, are in Chinese. I can't read Chinese but my memories are in the universal language of gratitude.

Going for the Seven Summits

No matter how high I climb, I always have to climb back down to reality at some point.

Despite my successful first attempt on Everest, I didn't think of myself as a mountaineer. Rather I was an ordinary game-ranger who wanted to climb Everest, get to the top and end my adventure there.

I was certain as I descended from that summit, that I wouldn't be venturing into such cold, dangerous places again.

But, after a while I realised that Everest was not just a climb. And it was also not the only way for me to promote mountaineering in Africa.

Mountains, mountaineering and adventuring had become my addiction, and now I often find myself planning the next expedition before I even begin the current one.

Although sometimes I start to feel lost as soon as I come back to reality, my beloved family helps me to settle down between trips. I need to provide for them, and that keeps me from becoming too adventurous.

Now, of course, I'm pursuing my goal to become the first black African to climb all Seven Summits ... the highest mountains on each of the seven continents.

Aconcagua (6959 metres), Argentina, South America – 2006

This was to be the third of the seven summits that I attempted, since I already had Everest (2003) and Kilimanjaro (1999) under my belt.

I joined a commercial expedition for the climb – Jagged Globe, again – on what is known as the most unpredictable of the seven summits.

After the usual system of acclimatisation climbs, we set off for our summit bid on a rather brilliant day, a rare experience on this mountain.

I was so fired up that I never looked back; the biggest motivation was that I was missing my family, as I had not spoken to them for fifteen days.

Once on top of the highest peak in the southern hemisphere, I took a few photographs, sang the national anthem, and then prayed for my family.

Thank you John, as always, for helping finance this climb for me.

Elbrus (5642 metres), Russia, Europe – 2006

By the time my bags were packed and all my papers in place, almost a year had passed from when I first started organising the trip.

Our guide, Vladimir, offered a short refresher course on ice climbing and the use of crampons – and for the first time I discovered that I was more experienced than my team-mates.

It wasn't long before I achieved what I had set out to do – and I stood on the top of Europe's highest at exactly 12.30 pm Russian time. I dropped to my knees in tears.

This was my fourth of the seven summits, and the second for my team mates, who were also going for all seven.

The three days in Moscow before I returned home was spent indoors, as I was really fed up with the place. But I had done what I had set out to do, and that thought brought all the joy and happiness to me.

Carstensz Pyramid (4 884 metres), New Guinea, Oceania – 2006

Carstensz Pyramid was the fifth of the seven summits, again thanks to John. I once again joined a commercial expedition, this time Adventure Peaks. There just two clients and one leader.

We got to the top in bad weather, although it was indeed a fantastic climb. The experience was really scary for me, as I am not at all a rock climber!

Vinson (4 892 metres), Antarctica – 2006

On 13 December 2006 I flew from Johannesburg to Cape Town, to Buenos Aires to Santiago to Punta Arenas in Chile.

Vinson is the second-most expensive mountain to climb after Everest. This was to be my first expedition with only two in the team: Alex Harris and myself and, within seven days of leaving home, I was once again on top of the world with joy!

The lesson for me during this climb was the importance of capitalising on every available opportunity, banking on the now because the morrow may never come.

Denali (McKinley) (6 194 metres), Alaska, North America – 2007 attempt

In May 2007 I joined a commercial expedition to Denali (also known as Mount McKinley), but persistent bad weather saw my dream of climbing all the seven summits remain just that: a dream.

It had taken a lot of hard work, sacrifice and time to get to Denali; it was already a good two years of effort by the time our team leader announced that we would be going down.

My heart sank. All that stood between me and my dream was deep snow, limited visibility and cold wind. We had climbed to the highest camp and all that we needed was eight hours of calm.

At Base Camp I looked back towards the mountain, and realised that even though I did not make it this time, the mountain will always be there, waiting to be climbed. I could still return, and I will. I will finish that which I began.

About the writers

In September 2006 Sibusiso was honoured by President Thabo Mbeki with the National Order of Ikhamanga for his inspiring and outstanding achievements in the field of mountaineering.

On 17 January 2008, Sibusiso and his Harmony Gold Team Extreme partner, Alex Harris, became the first South Africans to reach the South Pole after walking 1 100 kilometres across the snow and ice, unassisted and unsupported.

Sibusiso has set out to join the Seven Summits club. Currently (March 2008) there are just five South Africans amongst 198 members. He is planning a new attempt on Denali in 2008.

Sibusiso has competed in the Dusi canoe marathon and founded a running club, Born to Win. Sibusiso is also the African ambassador for the Free Play Foundation. When he is not on one of his adventures, or in Johannesburg or Swaziland, Sibusiso lives with his family in Nelspruit.

Gail Jennings is a writer based in Cape Town. After the cold and blizzards drove her off her second summit (Elbrus), she decided she preferred to read and write about mountains instead, and spend more time on her mountain bike.